The Trout Dreams

THE TROUT DREAMS

A true romance of fly-fishing in New Zealand

DEREK
GRZELEWSKI

STACKPOLE
BOOKS
Guilford, Connecticut

Published by Stackpole Books
An imprint of The Rowman & Littlefield Publishing Group, Inc.
4501 Forbes Boulevard, Suite 200, Lanham, Maryland 20706
www.rowman.com

Distributed by NATIONAL BOOK NETWORK

First published in 2019 by David Bateman Ltd,
Unit 2/5 Workspace Drive, Hobsonville, Auckland, New Zealand
www.batemanpublishing.co.nz

Text and photography © Derek Grzelewski, 2019
Typographical design © David Bateman Ltd, 2019

All rights reserved. No part of this book may be reproduced in any form or by any electronic or mechanical means, including information storage and retrieval systems, without written permission from the publisher, except by a reviewer who may quote passages in a review.

British Library Cataloguing in Publication Information available

Library of Congress Cataloging-in-Publication Data available

ISBN: 978-0-8117-1452-5 (paperback)

Book design: Nick Turzynski, redinc. Book Design, Auckland
Cover artwork: Diane Michelin
Author photograph: Ross Mackay, Stash Media Worx
All photography by Derek Grzelewski
except colour section 1, page 3: Casey Cravens; colour section 2, page 6, image 1: Fish & Game New Zealand
Quotation sources: Page 7 Izaak Walton, *The Compleat Angler* (Richard Marriot, London, 1653); Edward Abbey, as quoted from a speech to environmentalists in Missoula, Montana, and Colorado, published in *High Country News* Vol.8, No.19 (24 September 1976); Jerome K. Jerome, *Three Men in a Boat* (J.W. Arrowsmith Ltd, Bristol, London, 1889).

∞™ The paper used in this publication meets the minimum requirements of American National Standard for Information Sciences—Permanence of Paper for Printed Library Materials, ANSI/NISO Z39.48-1992.

Printed in China by Everbest Printing Co. Ltd

contents

To Jennifer, for being you . . .

'Study to be quiet.'

IZAAK WALTON

'Do not burn yourselves out. Be as I am — a reluctant enthusiast . . . a part-time crusader, a half-hearted fanatic. Save the other half of yourselves and your lives for pleasure and adventure. It is not enough to fight for the land; it is even more important to enjoy it. While you can. While it's still here.'

EDWARD ABBEY

'Let your boat of life be light, packed with only what you need — a homely home and simple pleasures, one or two friends, worth the name, someone to love and someone to love you, a dog, and a pipe or two, enough to eat and enough to wear, and a little more than enough to drink; for thirst is a dangerous thing.'

JEROME K. JEROME

'Your casting is poetry in motion, mine is more like punk rock.'

JENNIFER WHITE

prologue

THE BIG TROUT HELD just under the tongue of current breaking off an island-like boulder and from where we stood it was nearly invisible, camouflaged beneath the liquid greenstone of the river frothed with white water. Only the sway of its tail gave it away, and only when a brief window of smooth water passed over it, which was how I first sighted the brute.

'There is a good fish just down and left of that boulder,' I said to my companion Frank Mosley, and pointed to it with my fly rod.

Frank couldn't see it, but this was to be expected. Unless you've trained your eyes to spot New Zealand trout, you are likely to miss all but the most obvious ones. Frank was from Montana, accustomed to fishing water rather than individual trout, though to his credit it was tough to see fish here in the Reefton backcountry. The ostrich-egg boulders that cobble the riverbeds are bone-white and, in bright sunlight, as hard on the eyes as the blinding glare of a glacier.

'Trust me,' I said. 'There is a fish there all right, and a big one too. Just cast a metre up and left of that boulder.'

Frank did, even if he was not entirely convinced. His cast was accurate enough, but for a long, suspended moment nothing happened. He lifted the rod and the line seemed snagged.

'Damn, I caught the botto. . .,' he said, but then the bottom near the boulder exploded with a fury of spray. The big trout was airborne above it, shaking its head from side to side, its arched wet body glinting gold as it caught the sunlight. The fish bounced off the water a couple of times, then shot downstream, like a soft lithe torpedo and a contradiction to all laws of fluid mechanics.

'Oh, my Gawd,' Frank's voice was an octave above his usual baritone. 'Did you see THAT? It's a monster!'

We followed at a run, rod held high but bent into a deep C, Frank's eyes fixed at the end of his line. He seemed in a trance, ready to walk on water. Well, almost. He was fit and nimble for his mid-sixties, but a few times I had to catch and steady him as he stumbled over rocks he did not see. The fish was taking us down the river and we crossed and recrossed the tumbling current, wrestling with it, tripping and fumbling on the slippery bottom, gaining some line, losing it again, but at all times keeping it taut like a guitar string.

Twice Frank was down on his knees, flailing, on all threes but with his rod arm steady and strong. With a pang of dread, I saw where the fish was heading: a mother of all logjams in a pool

The big trout was airborne above it, shaking its head from side to side, its arched wet body glinting gold as it caught the sunlight.

below us. If he went in there, into the debris of past floods, we would never get him out.

But then, in the eye of calm below the rapids and just short of the logjam, I finally netted the fish and he was just shy of the magic 10 lbs that is the hallmark of a trophy. Frank got his pictures and we released the fish immediately. He was a magnificent trout in its prime, with a fiercely hooked lower jaw, muscled body and a glistening skin that seemed too tight for it.

He was just as spent as we were, and he nosed into a rock in the slack water right at our feet, and for a long while all three of us just sat there in absolute stillness, catching our breaths, the only sound the murmur of the river.

Then I heard that Frank was sobbing – and trying to cover it with laughter. He rubbed his eyes with his buff, his hands trembling. 'The goddamned river water got into my eyes,' he said, but he was fooling no one.

I smiled and said it was a really good fish, the kind you'd expect out here.

'No, no, you don't understand. I've been fishing all my life, since I was big enough to hold a rod, and this is the best trout I have ever caught,' Frank cut in. 'Where I live you cannot even buy this kind of experience any more, no matter how much money you have.'

He fell quiet and withdrawn afterwards, taking time to absorb the experience, and he did not want to fish any more that day, as if not to dilute the quality with repetition or numbers.

On the way back down the river he said:

'You're probably spoilt because you can have this anytime you want, but for me this one fish was worth coming all the way down here for. Mountain climbers go to the Himalayas for the best there is, fly fishermen come to New Zealand. Today, I bagged my personal Everest.'

Yep, you've guessed it: I was back to guiding and it happened in a most roundabout kind of way. Ever since *The Trout Diaries* was published in 2011, and even more so after *The Trout Bohemia* two years later, I've been receiving a steady flow of emails from the readers, an unexpected perk and delight from writing books. (When you write for magazines, whether local or international, as I had for the past two and a half decades, most commonly the only reader feedback you get is when you make a mistake – a trivial gaffe or a factual error – which a certain kind of person just loves to point out, though rarely in a constructive or humorous way.)

But these letters were different. Often they were deeply personal since, at its best and true, fly-fishing is a profound and intimate experience, and, yes, they were also filled with accounts of the writers' own river exploits, both happy and less so, and they carried a common message that somehow we fished in similar ways and for compatible reasons, responding as if by resonance to the call of the trout waters. The authors of the emails wanted me to know that they got what I was trying to convey in my own writing about the magic of fly-fishing that defies explanations and is so hard to put into words, or, as Hemingway said, it's just plain 'too swell to talk about'.

More often than not, the emails would conclude with something like 'I wish we could go for a fish together one day' to which I routinely replied that I was busy but my guide friends, some of whom were featured in the books, could certainly help with that.

Then, one time, after an email exchange with a particularly insistent reader, I thought 'why the hell not?'. I was about to leave on a week-long trout hunt and so was he, and in the same region. The fishing was good, the forecast even better. Our dates matched; it was too much of a coincidence.

We met, and fished, and camped, and talked long into the campfire nights about all manner of things. For the first time guiding did not feel like drudgery to me, an exercise in miracle-making against all odds and lack of even the most fundamental skills that need to be tactfully endured at the time, and later washed off with copious amounts of whisky.

To the contrary, the outing turned out to be one of the most memorable fishing trips I've ever been on largely because I'd changed the way I guided — changing not the *what* but the *how*. The mechanics remained the same, but the attitude was different, and the attitude is like tinted glasses: it can darken or brighten how you see things and colour your perception. And so instead of trying to guarantee saleable goods — usually trout and ideally big trout and plenty of it — in the process attempting to control the uncontrollable and getting stressed about it all, I began to guide the way I fished for myself.

Walking the rivers, looking for and finding fish, taking shots at them to the best of my ability and seeing how this played out, celebrating when it did, laughing when it didn't. Essentially, going fishing with clients as I would with friends, just giving them all the opportunities. This made for a much more relaxed atmosphere, reducing the pressure that so often both the guide and the guided angler put on themselves. After all, fly-fishing was meant to be fun, right? Wasn't this one of the reasons why we did it?

In a way then, this was a return to what fly-fishing was supposed to be, at least in its pure and true form, before it has been subjected to rampant commercialisation which has turned trout into a commodity to be advertised, acquired, shown off and bragged about. As American fly-fishing author John Gierach wrote with his trademark sarcasm, the kind of people he'd want to guide didn't usually want a guide or to be guided. Somehow, though, the second time around I managed to find the middle way of doing what I loved without pimping it out. I guess my books have acted as a filter and a declaration of intent, style and approach, so that I did not attract wannabes who just wanted to catch big fish only to post pictures of them on Facebook, but rather true anglers who engage with the world of trout through fly-fishing and on deeper levels, more like my own.

This change in attitude of treating guiding not as a job but as a way of taking new friends out fishing and helping to make things happen for them took time to grow and evolve. It has been both radical and revelatory, although I cannot claim to be the originator. I had a friend who was a mountain guide, one of the most experienced in the country. We used to fish and ski tour together a lot, and one time he told me that for him it did not make any difference whether he was guiding a client or climbing with a friend; he was getting just as much enjoyment out of both.

Anton died guiding Aoraki/Mt Cook some years ago, but his words have stayed with me ever since. Finally, I think, I too *got* what he was trying to tell me. Perhaps I'd grown up a little as well.

And a good thing I did, because otherwise I might have never met Jennifer.

A few years had passed since I lived and wrote *The Trout Bohemia*. Ella, the book's main protagonist and its chief villain, was long gone. Last time I heard anything about her she was studying tango in Buenos Aires and no doubt had taken her demons there with her. After the endless dramas and emotional fireworks of trying to be with her, I delighted in silences and the peace that followed after she was gone. They were like a clearing after a storm, quiet enough so that I could hear the sound of rivers again, and so I wrote, and I fished through the seasons and ski toured the winter backcountry with my dog Maya and only a few of the closest friends. I thought if this was all that there ever was, it was fine by me and certainly enough and fulfilling. But Life does not let you idle for long and new events of the highest magnitude were already approaching my horizon even if I could not quite see them yet.

Like Frank and so many others, Jennifer wrote to me asking about fishing in New Zealand. She had read my books and she was intrigued by them and by the challenge of trying to catch those almost mythical antipodean trout, the style we favoured and its self-imposed purity.

'I'm a simple Colorado girl who just loves to fly fish and doesn't care about catching,' she wrote, and I thought 'Yeah, right. They all say that, until you get them to the river and point out trout bigger than anything they've ever seen.'

All this was happening during the busy peak season and so I wrote back to her with some hasty suggestions, all of which were long-shot and rather expensive options, at least a year away, and so I fully expected not to hear back from her. Surprisingly, she replied the very next day; she was positively dreaming about New Zealand trout. I wrote back, and so did she again, and before long we had a conversation going, then daily messages, then the first phone call and a video chat.

I was taken by her enthusiasm. She had never fished in New Zealand, but she'd clocked an impressive fly-fishing mileage elsewhere, as diverse as it was exotic. British Columbia steelhead and salmon, Christmas Island bonefish, tarpon and snook in Mexico and Florida, redfish in Louisiana, and trout, wherever she could find them. In her family, fly-fishing went back four generations and she lived near one of the best trout waters in America: the Fryingpan and the Roaring Fork rivers near their confluence with the upper Colorado.

Her father Brit, retired to a riverside property, fished most days and when he didn't he tied flies, exquisitely crafted and just as innovative, and they spent many happy river days together, reunited by their mutual passion for trout after years of estrangement and living in different countries and cultures.

One thing too was clear, that unlike so many fishing wives, girlfriends or daughters dragged into the sport against their will but enduring it just to please their loved ones, Jennifer's interest in fly-fishing was pure and independent, unadulterated by influences and peer pressure.

'I love it all, all aspects of it,' she told me in one of our earlier conversations, 'the fishing, the fish, the bugs, messing about with the gear, thinking about it, reading about it, dreaming about it. Fly water is where I'm the happiest, and all I need to know is that there are fish in it and that there's possibility of catching some of them.'

I was intrigued. The season flew by — the cicada summer, autumn mayfly hatches, the first spawning runs of early winter — and my days were often long and demanding. Yet every time I got home, every morning I'd get ready to head out to the river again, there would be a little message from Jennifer — a note of few words, a picture or an e-card, a link to a song or a movie clip, a joke or a flirt. Before she went fishing for steelhead on the Dean River with her father, for a week at a remote fly-in camp and totally out of cell and Wi-Fi range, she mailed me a pack of home-made postcards with a detailed instruction what to open on what day and in which order. Thus, in our communications, she never missed a day and, as I replied in kind, I also thought 'This chick is not just keen on fishing; she's got some staying power too'.

But all is glitz and glam and endless optimism in the digital world where everything seems possible and our minds fill in the blanks with more of what we want to see. After months of living in this cyberspace bubble of trout fishing romance we felt ready for a real-life encounter. 'We should meet' became our standing joke and a sign-off line. By early New Zealand winter, we started to hatch a plan.

She wanted to come for a week and I thought it was an awfully long way to travel here and back for just a few days of fishing. 'Look, why don't you come for at least a couple of weeks,' I suggested. 'I'll guide you for the first few days because you'll definitely need it, and from then on we can fish like friends, see if our trout dreams match, and how everything else falls into place.' She said yes, but as we continued to talk our dreams and make plans it soon became apparent that even two weeks did not seem anywhere near enough. 'Why don't we just jump in at the deep end? Make it two months if you dare,' I suggested, and to my greatest surprise Jennifer again said yes.

She booked her air ticket for late October. That winter at the Southern Lakes was one of the best ever, with an abundance of snow and sunny still weather, and so I was out ski touring every good day, sending Jennifer little movie clips of our ski runs, or chatting with her live from the mountain summits whenever cell reception allowed. Then the trout season started and I was back to River X, on my annual early-season pilgrimage, and every day I drove out of the valley and into reception so we could chat and reconnect.

'Maybe we should send the Apple people some champagne or single malt with a thank-you note,' we joked, 'as without them this transcontinental trout romance could never be possible.'

After so many hours and terabytes of data it felt as if we had known each other forever and now, like kids before Christmas, we were counting days: 14 . . . 10 . . . 5 . . . 3 . . .

But with growing excitement also came matching anxiety. Could we really do this? Could we truly live the trout bohemia dream of doing what we love with someone we love, finding a kind of trout soulmate in each other? And, could we face the disappointments of failure should our visions and dreams come crashing down?

What if this whole crazy plan did not work out? On the other hand, what if it did?

We were about to unplug from the digital reality, meet in real life for the first time, and find out.

chapter 1

A COUPLE OF DAYS before the season's opening I was doing a talk at the local library. When you write trout books for a living, these kinds of gigs come with the territory. About forty people turned up, some blokes already wearing their camo gear, burning with opening-day fever, eager for some last-minute tips and secrets which the library staff had promised in their posters.

I did deliver on that promise, though not in the way the crowd may have expected.

'You've probably come here hoping for some magic formulas and strategies or catch-all flies which no trout can refuse,' I said, 'but I have a tip for you that is by far more valuable than any of that.'

Pause. You've got to love this kind of silence.

'If there is one single thing you can do to improve your fly-fishing it's to put some quality time into your casting.'

There was a palpable sense of disappointment in the crowd, a kind of 'is that it?' deflation. But I ploughed on.

'When you're a hunter, you wouldn't dream of going after a trophy animal without putting in some serious shooting practice on the range, to get used to the trajectories and recoil, spreads and distances,' I said. 'The whole action needs to become automatic, programmed into your muscle memory through repetition. I mean, you don't want to be stalking a deer all day and then, when you finally get a clear shot at it, raising your rifle and going "Where is the safety on this thing again?" And yet in fly-fishing this is all too common.'

Strange as it seems, even many of the self-declared lifelong anglers, people for whom fly-fishing is their deepest passion, have never quite taken the time to learn to cast properly, I went on. In fact, until the fairly recent revolution and the arrival on the scene of people like Stu Tripney and Carl McNeil, the first two master instructors in this country, there was no real tradition of casting well in New Zealand.

In true pioneering DIY spirit, the most common scenario would have been that, during your introduction to the sport, someone — your father, uncle or a friend — showed you how to cast. 'This is how you do it: hold the rod like this and just flick it out and, there, you're fishing.'

From that moment on, it was assumed that you could cast. Sadly, this was also when your learning had stopped.

This is not only a New Zealanders' predicament. Ask any professional guide and they'll tell you: their main, and often only, concern is whether or not their clients can cast well enough. Talk is cheap, assurances shallow, and 'I've been fishing all my life' only raises eyebrows and suspicion. Those first few casts on a river are a tell-all, a decider whether a guide can relax into just being a guide, or whether he has to put on his magician's hat and try to conjure up miracles.

I told them about the American guiding legend Flip Pallot, who talked with brutal honesty about 'the last forty feet', about how anglers travelled partway around the world and spent thousands on flights, gear, guides and lodges, only to fall apart on the last forty feet — the cast that separated them from their dream fish. Pallot was talking about salt water, mainly tarpon and bonefish which were his speciality, but in the case of New Zealand trout, though the distance was similar, the precision and the quality of the cast needed to be doubled.

From the expressions on the faces in the crowd I could see I was getting some traction. One guy even asked how to go about relearning to cast.

Get an orange line, I told him, specifically for practice, a long-belly distance line like the LOOP Opti 210 or an equivalent, so that you can see the shapes of your loops and learn how to change and control them. You may also consider investing in a yarn rod — it looks like a Walmart toy but is in fact a precisely balanced tool, particularly good in learning how to make crisper stops and tighter loops.

Find some quality instruction, ideally in person. Books are good, but videos are better. I mentioned a few titles and people were taking notes now, always a good sign.

Set up a practice rod, I went on, with that orange line, leader and brightly coloured yarn for a fly (Glo Bug tying material is ideal). Above all, and most important, practise away from the river and the fish. You will not improve your casting by fishing, the way you don't learn music by playing pieces but scales and exercises instead. When you focus on those, with time you'll notice your pieces improve. So do your scales with the fly rod on the grass: pickups and laydowns, stops and loops, slow and fast, forward, back and sideways, hauls and no hauls, roll casts and Speys . . .

In the front row an elderly gentleman — another lifelong angler — cleared his throat and, with the air of finality, declared: 'You can't roll cast on the grass!'

I did not want to embarrass the old chap so I smiled and segued into the casting principles: no line slack, straight rod tip path, the timing of pauses, sizes of casting strokes and power application. If the guy was not open to new ideas and ready for change, it wasn't my job to convert him. As the Dalai Lama once said: 'If you talk, you only repeat what you know; if you listen you may actually learn something new.'

So, where is your casting at? How accurate are you, how consistent? Can you lay down a straight line and leader every time in that critical forty to forty-five foot (12–15 m) range? Can you cast into a moderate headwind, know how to avoid hooking yourself when the wind blows across your body? Does your line land on the water like a spider web or more like a falling tree? Does it drag and if so, do you know what to do about it, and not spook the fish in the process?

Years ago, I hesitate to say how many, I was fishing the Tongariro with Paul Arden, Mr Sexyloops and self-proclaimed 'most expensive casting instructor in the world'. Paul had cast to a sighted fish with impeccable accuracy, and the line was drifting down without a hint of drag towards a snag which protruded from the water like some witch's crooked talon.

With perfect timing, Paul made the tiniest of flicks with his wrist and an omega-shaped loop slithered off the rod tip and travelled down the line, clearing the snag at just the right moment, gracefully dissipating beyond it. The line continued its perfect drift; the fly never moved. The fish took, ran and promptly wrapped itself around the said talon. It was fair game, though, and the first time I saw just the kind of magic that can be conjured up with a fly rod in skilled hands.

With such inspiration, in my own fly-fishing journey I have relearnt to cast several times, most notably by spending several days with Stu Tripney, as I described in *The Trout Bohemia*, and most recently, by preparing for international casting exams. I'm sure the trout do not recognise such qualifications and, in any case, sailing through the exams was only the proverbial cherry on top. What mattered most were the several months of steady and almost daily practice — sometimes only minutes, other times up to an hour or more.

As the Dalai Lama once said: 'If you talk, you only repeat what you know; if you listen you may actually learn something new.'

What I can relate from this experience is that casting becomes a most enjoyable pursuit in and of itself, and it reveals its nuances to you step by step, and only when you are ready, when you start asking the right questions, do you begin to develop the finesse and the touch.

The journey is like climbing a mountain ridge: there are ups and downs and plateaux. There are false summits, too, milestones of accomplishment, which though satisfying, only reveal that there is further to go.

Can you ever get to the top? Few people have, and those who have got near it appear to embrace the old Zen credo: 'when you reach the top of the mountain, keep climbing'. So the journey never needs to end.

Will it help you catch more and bigger fish? For sure, though only to a point. At first, your learning curve will be almost vertical, but after a time you'll reach a plateau beyond which you will only catch fish in better style, not necessary more frequently.

How do you know when you're there? When on a sighted fish, you're confident you can get a fly to it with the first cast. Or the second cast, if you made the first one deliberately short to judge the distance, angles and drift. To use that hunting analogy again, when going after a trout, you've become a sniper and stopped being a hopeful machine-gunner.

I had one such epiphany recently while willow-grubbing in Southland. It was a perfect day, sunny and still, with a trickle of mayflies and consistently rising trout. I'd picked off a few fish already and then came across the willow-grub 'hatch'.

Willow grubs are a summer phenomenon, the larvae of willow gall sawfly, *Pontania proxima*, a relative of bees, ants and wasps. Not much is known about them, at least in the angling world, but for their unmistakable riverside appearance — the red blisters about the size of a coffee bean — which break out on willow leaves and often in such profusion, from a distance, they can affect the hue of entire trees, from the usual vivid green to dull russet. Inside the blisters or galls are tiny caterpillar-like larvae, yellow or lime-green with black heads, and only about six millimetres long, and when triggered by the summer heat they emerge en masse, with good numbers of them falling into the river below. When this happens, trout tend to lock on to this 'hatch', obsessively and to the point of ignoring all other food, big or small. The tiny grubs, curved into crescents and suspended on top of the surface film, must be to trout like the equivalent of caviar floating down the feed lines, one grain at a time.

Since the grub fall from the trees, and the fish are almost always underneath the branches, you often need to side-cast and with fair accuracy as the trout won't move much out of their narrow feed lines. There is only one fly you need in such times — Stu Tripney's 'banana', a sliver of yellow foam tied crescent-shaped on a #16 or #18 hook — so it all is down to casting.

I got a couple of easy fish downstream of the willows, but as I moved up I became aware of another one, hogging the prime lie. I heard him slurping several times and it took a long moment of stillness and intense looking to locate him.

He was in an impossible position, only his nose protruding from a thicket of trailing willow branches and the window of clear drift was no more than a couple of feet long, with more greenery above and in front. But he was feeding with abandon, an irresistible sight.

I waded out slowly, mindful of the wake, measured out the line and cast. I don't know how it happened, I probably could not do it again, but on that first cast everything went just right. The fish took, panicked and swam forward a couple of feet into the open, and with rod-tip-to-the-knuckles side pressure I did not let him go into the thicket again.

I released him and stopped fishing for the day. It felt as if all the practice I'd ever done went into that one cast. It was my own glimpse of mastery, a 'Paul Arden' moment, and I wanted to savour it, and make it last, even if more fish were probably still rising upstream of me.

If fly-fishing is your passion, if you love trout and where and how they live, take a good honest look at your casting, and then get down to work on it. There is always room to improve. You will not only catch more fish but enjoy the sport all the more, perhaps edging towards making it more an art than just putting some Omega-3 on the table. Watch some clips of the best casters, people like Christopher Rownes, they will redefine your ideas of what is possible with a fly rod and what casting can look like.

Few words of caution from a fellow journeyman though: don't try to figure it out by yourself. Get help. Some of the finer points of casting are subtle and may escape you unless properly explained and shown, so you may end up practising mistakes. And bad habits are harder to get out of than new ones are to acquire.

Finally, don't go for distance! When you get a few guys casting together, in no time more and more line comes off the reels and the practice becomes a messy competition of who can cast further, complete with fly lines landing in crumpled heaps and sore shoulders.

In New Zealand, you rarely need to cast far and it's more important to be accurate than to lob out the entire fly line. Also, distance casting exaggerates all the faults so, again, you may end up just reinforcing your errors. Pull in the line and see how far you can cast while maintaining good form. This is your starting point, and the distance will come in its own time. Experts make distance casting appear effortless. It definitely should not look like an exercise in shot put.

So, 'you can't roll cast on the grass?' Really? Want me to show you? How long do you want it? With haul or without? And have you seen a Snake Roll yet?

When I first saw her at the airport she wore flowing bell-bottom yoga pants, a pink blouse and a touch of make-up matched by plenty of indigenous jewellery, and the only hint that she could be an angler coming for a two-month-long trout safari were two enormous green Orvis duffel bags she trundled through the Arrivals lobby and the Smith polaroids that held up her long blonde hair like a headband.

We hugged like long lost friends, reunited. It was the oddest sensation to meet for the first time even though we felt like we had known each other well.

She had an easy confident manner and laughed freely.

'We only knew each other by letter [when] I went to meet her off the train.' She hummed into my ear the opening of 'Prairie Wedding' by Mark Knopfler, the favourite song that had become somewhat prophetic of our story.

'Better hand you up on the wagon and drive up the home trail,' I said, bastardising the lyrics some more.

At the back of the camper, Maya gave Jennifer an enthusiastic welcome, not yet aware that our family pack was about to undergo a major reshuffle. An hour later we were walking the high bank of my home river and I was pointing out to Jennifer several large brown trout happily rising down below, their bodies glinting bronze and copper in the overhead sunlight. These fish are so habituated to an almost daily angler disturbance they are pretty much uncatchable and better treated as river ornaments than honest quarry. But Jennifer did not know that yet and so her eyes, though tired from jet lag, lit up with wonder.

A few days later, after several more hand-in-hand dog walks, candle-light dinners and some non-digital tête-à-tête we had so long promised ourselves, we loaded up the camper and headed out for our first trout trip together. We were in the cloud-nine daze of beginning this two-month-long blind date and everything was working out better than we had imagined. But we knew that fishing together would be the crux, a maker or a breaker of it all because we both loved it so much, and we had fished alone, with our dogs, for too long and we dreamed of doing it with someone more than a friend, someone who truly *got* our ways and sensitivities, someone who did it for similar reasons and, ideally, at a compatible level.

Having heard plenty of her fishing stories I was upbeat and confident; sure, some adjustments may be needed, and I was more than willing to make these, but as we neared the river Jennifer grew perceivably apprehensive though she hid it well with smiles and chit-chat. Until we got to the river.

'I should warn you again,' she said there, 'I've made more than a few guides want to jump into the water and drown themselves out of frustration.'

'Why?'

'Errr . . . You'll see.' An uneasy smile.

'Trust me, I've seen some bad fishing, like the worst ever. If you guide long enough, you pretty much see it all, so I don't think you can surprise me.'

She was silent on that one. Then, as we rigged up ready to go, she said:

'Just remember, whatever happens, I love it more than anything, but I really don't care about catching fish.'

She gave me a peck on a cheek and added, 'Well, if my fishing really sucks you can always take me back to the airport.' Just then, looking over her shoulder, I saw the first trout. It was hugging the bank, sheltering from the current behind a clump of turf: lithe, sleek and muscular, maybe seven pounds. Maybe more.

This, I thought, for anyone, would be a tough introduction to fly-fishing in New Zealand.

It was still early season but also a long weekend and though there were closer and fishier places to go they would also be a lot busier and so I strategised that this West Coast river would be a better option. At least we should have the place to ourselves. And that we did.

'It's not an ideal place for you to start; the fishing is always hard here, maybe too hard,' I tried to keep my guide's commentary light if honest, 'but the fish are big and every one is worth catching so let's just see how you go.'

I could see that this was not helping, but we started anyway.

Jennifer scared off the first few fish without ever getting an honest chance. She slapped a couple of casts down as if to whip the fish, overshot the next one by three metres to the same effect, she got hung up in the bushes above one trout, spooked another by getting too close to it. She tangled even before getting the line out and let rocks tumble down into the water ahead of her approach — in a word, made all the usual mistakes of a New Zealand trout neophyte. Her excitement and pressure were paralysing her, although, as I said, the fish were big and in slow glassy water, a fair challenge for even the most skilled of anglers.

As the day went on and I tried to keep the mood light, the line from the instructional video, which we had so enjoyed the night before departure and which was made by my friend and Fiordland guide Dean Bell, became a summary of each of her efforts.

'The fish is long gone but Jennifer doesn't know that yet.'

She was yet to come up with the question New Zealand guides hear most often, after their client bungled the cast: 'Is he still there?' She was getting increasingly exasperated, even though I kept assuring her she was doing better than most.

It was then that we came across a good-sized fish nymphing in fast broken water in a riffle formed by a diagonally sunken log. There were no obstacles and no other technicalities and Jennifer's loops for once were clean and crisp, and accurate enough, the sunken log a guideline along which to cast. On about the fourth or fifth fly change the white tuft of her indicator bobbed down violently and for a heart-sinking moment I thought she had snagged on the log.

But then I heard her scream, a long excited *aaaaaaah!*, rising in pitch, a sound that — like the whir of a treasured reel — was soon to become one of my most beloved sounds in the whole world. She was on, and next to the log the fish churned the water into froth, angry and surprised, though luckily not tearing off downstream, into the backing and the logjams below as trout often do on this river.

Nothing went wrong, the knots and the fly held and I netted the fish at Jennifer's feet, and though we both detest 'grip 'n' grin' mug shots we took a few, for her father, and for her, because after all it was her first ever New Zealand trout, caught in 'experts-only' water and it weighed a solid five pounds.

She was drunk with elation and to prolong the high we stopped fishing for the day and found a place to camp on an empty beach, the steady sea breeze blowing away the sandflies. There was plenty of driftwood and I built a campfire, and we sat in foldable chairs facing the sea, holding hands and drinking bourbon, watching the stars come up over the horizon. I'd been here many times before, and caught plenty of fish, some real big ones too, but I had never been so happy and contented, and I told Jennifer that because girls like to hear such things.

'Awww! You mean it? Really? It's so sweet! I loved fishing with you; it was the best day ever,' she crooned.

'You did so well today, so well!' I praised her. 'It takes most people days to tune into fishing here, no matter how good they think they are. And you got there in a day; that's amazing. And you know what? Tomorrow will be even better.'

We stayed out long into the night, savouring the contentment and this newly found togetherness. And a good thing we did because 'tomorrow' would turn out to be a disaster.

The day was calm but overcast, the visibility less than ideal. Still, using the Ignitor lenses, high banks and backdrop of trees I was finding fish right from the start. But spotting trout, though hard, was the easy part. It was Jennifer's casting that was a shock to everyone: me, herself and especially the trout. The day before she had had some good and bad moments, but today it was as if she had never cast before.

She was rushing everything, her timing was all out, there was no accuracy worth mentioning.

'Your casting is poetry in motion, mine is more like punk rock,' she tried to make light of it, but the joke fell flat, and she knew it. The locale and the calibre of our quarry called for stealth and precision, a tiptoeing approach of a bow hunter, not casting to the rhythm of the Sex Pistols. As it was, she may as well have been throwing rocks at the fish; the effect would have been the same.

We persevered well into the afternoon, but it wasn't getting any better. There wasn't even anything to correct, the whole thing just totally fell apart and the more frustrated she got with herself, the worse her casting became.

I was getting increasingly quiet and withdrawn, thinking to myself, 'If you want to fish with me you'd better lift your game, like several orders of magnitude, because this is just too painful to watch.' Only last night, I had visions of us travelling the length of the country, following the seasons and the trout calendar I so love to live by. But not fishing like this. We had covered several kilometres of the river, seen a good number of fish and we never got anywhere near engaging with one. Staying at the beach would have been just as productive, and a lot more fun.

Finally, after Jennifer piled up most of her fly line on top of another large trout, sending it off at blurring speed for the cover of the opposite bank, I could not hold back any more.

'For god's sake, Jen, show these fish some respect,' I said and instantly regretted it.

'I'm sorry, I don't know what's happened.' I saw she was close to tears. 'Seems I've totally lost it today.'

'Today?'

'Well, I warned you! I have this thing: some days I can fish like a pro, other days I'm like a never-ever. I don't know why or what's causing it; seeing all these huge fish and you standing next to me certainly doesn't help. I don't handle the pressure to perform very well and this always drives my guides crazy.'

'You said you were an actress in Mexico? In Spanish? Surely, there was no room for stage fright there, no?'

'Acting is easy, fishing to these monsters is not.'

I scanned the terrain up the river, there was more glassy water, technical casting, probably more wary trout.

'Look, there's really no point continuing like this,' I said. 'It's just not gonna happen. We're only pissing these fish off without ever getting an honest chance of catching any. I'd rather leave them undisturbed than fish to them like this.'

We turned around and started back downstream. The silence was awkward and within it you could almost hear the distant sounds of dreams come crashing down.

Partway down to the camper I thought: 'This fly-fishing can be such an emotional roller-coaster. It lets you experience the highest highs and the lowest lows, and all because of a fish. Crazy, isn't it?'

I said nothing, but I took Jennifer's hand, squeezed it in reassurance, and we walked back hand in hand just as we said we would. At least this part of the trout dream was working out.

'You taking me back to the airport?' she tried a smile.

'No, not yet, but we've got work to do. A lot of work.'

Back home, I set up a casting rod for her, with an orange line and a tuft of red wool for a fly, and we started a daily practice on the grass, first taking her casting apart to its foundation elements, cleaning these up, then putting it all back together again. I gave her several exercises and took videos of her casting on the phone so that she could see the difference between what she was doing and what she thought she was doing.

Within only a few days the gap had narrowed, though the issue of consistency would plague her for another year or so. It wasn't even the question of technique any more but of placing her full attention into what she was doing, especially when it mattered most, when the excitement and pressure to perform got in the way.

And of this non-Zen approach, her lack of laser-like focus, Jennifer was well aware. She told me how she frustrated the hell out of her steelhead guide on the Dean in British Columbia.

'"Why is my Snap T not working?" I asked him. He said, "Because you're not f***ing doing what I tell you to do."'

It all became a work in progress and would remain so for months to come, but meantime I started to put some targets out for her so that she could get to terms with the accuracy required to fish for New Zealand trout. One evening we were out for a quick after-dinner practice. Jen was casting to some empty wine bottles I'd spread out on the lawn for her and as I watched her I saw there were rabbits everywhere, dozens of them lounging around in the twilight, nibbling on grass, grooming or just chilling out, finding safety in numbers and the proximity of the nearby burrows. Even Maya did not bother them, in fact she seemed to just chill with them, almost as if she was looking after *her* rabbits, which was evident from her uncommon aggression towards any hawk coming near the place.

And so a thought occurred to me: why don't we use the rabbits for target practice?

There was one large buck lying on his front, side on towards us, his back legs fully stretched out behind him, maybe twelve or fifteen metres away, a realistic distance when sight-fishing for trout.

'Watch this,' I said to Jennifer, taking her rod.

I cast to him as you would to a trout — not directly at him but placing the red yarn a chosen distance in front of his nose. Five feet, three feet, then right in front of him. There was no reaction from the rabbit.

'Didn't spook,' I said, and cast directly at the critter.

The cast was a fraction long and so the leader landed over the rabbit's back legs, the red yarn a foot or so behind him. The line and the leader were straight and as I slowly drew them back towards me the red yarn was pulled over the rabbit's upturned foot and over his pads. The rabbit kicked his foot violently a couple of times, obviously tickled by the yarn, but otherwise he stayed where he was.

'This, my dear Jennifer, is what I'd call a *delicate presentation*.'

She laughed but got the idea. The era of punk-rock casting was coming to an end.

I had a long list of places and rivers I wanted to show her and fish together with her, some that I knew well, others that I had long wanted to explore, but it was clear that, in her evolution as an angler, Jennifer wasn't quite ready for them. There was no point walking for miles to look for large fish only to blow them off with careless or inaccurate casting. So I hatched a better plan, one that involved easy fish and a lot of them, though by Jennifer's Colorado standards each and every one would be a trophy.

Apart from casting, one other factor that hampered Jennifer's early fishing efforts with me was her inability to see all but the most obvious of trout. It wasn't really the matter of her vision, which is good, but more of tuning into a whole different way of looking, of teaching the eyes to see anew and with specialised focus.

In the world of trout, New Zealand has an unsurpassed reputation for sight-fishing: seeing the fish before it sees you, making an action plan for the best approach, sneaking into a position to make that all-important first cast and, if it all goes well up till there, experiencing that timeless moment of anticipation as the fly and the fish converge. It is intensely visual, an intimate and electrifying interaction with the fish, perhaps the most pure and satisfying way to engage with trout and as such the most sought-after angling adventure, sometimes at great effort and expense.

Yet most anglers inexperienced in this style of fishing, or unaccustomed to the clarity of water which makes it possible, frequently struggle to see fish, and when you point out to them one of the hard-to-see, perfectly camouflaged trout they think it is some kind of a practical joke. And keep in mind that usually the easier the fish are to see the harder they are to catch, not just because they can easily see you as well but because the easy-spotting water — glassy and slow — makes a stealthy presentation tough if not impossible. So, ideally, you want to start spotting those hard-to-see trout as they are more likely to be deceived, the broken surface which hides them also disguising any casting faux pas or drag and approach errors.

Where is your trout spotting at? Do you usually see plenty of fish or do you get frustrated with your inability and the rivers which seem lifeless? Do you find yourself spooking fish, seeing them too late or, worse, walking past them and having your companion point out that you just have, again and again?

At times, especially in less than ideal visibility, finding feeding fish may seem like an almost supernatural ability, but there is a method to the magic, and strategies, and you certainly do not need fish-eagle's eyes to find trout and create enough opportunities for a good day's fishing. So let's see if we can somewhat demystify the art of spotting trout.

Before you even start spotting fish, trying to X-ray the water and willing the trout to appear, you need to know where to look. Otherwise you'll end up straining your eyes through a lot of dead water, losing focus and enthusiasm, then spooking fish when you finally get to where they were feeding all along. Trout are not distributed evenly throughout a river; they prefer certain features and places, and learning to identify this prime trout real estate is the first skill to learn. The best way to do that is to begin looking at a river with the eyes of a paddler.

Notice how the river runs: how it turns from side to side, how the outside corner is always the deeper one, how there is usually a distinct staircase profile to the flow — pool, riffle, pool — and how the water speeds vary both along and across the river. These speed differences are the key features for a trout hunter. What you are looking for are current lines and shears — places where fast and slow water meet.

Trout are top predators and they do not needlessly exert themselves. Their preferred feeding spots are places where they can sit in slower water while feeding from the faster current. Browns are notorious for this, often parking up in totally slack water with just their noses edging into the current, and while the rainbows tend to favour faster flows, they still adhere to the same principles and behaviour. That is why you won't find trout feeding in strong featureless current. It simply takes too much of their energy just to stay in one place.

So look for any features and disturbances in the river flow: corners and bank protrusions, rocks and trees, current lines and seams. You'll soon see and realise that, because of the way the river flows, how pools funnel into riffles and turn left and right, the current lines are places where most of the waterborne trout food gets concentrated. They are the feed lines, and the edges of those are where you'll find most fish.

Of course, it's not all there is to it. A river is a complex three-dimensional environment, though looking down from above we perceive it only in 2-D. What we see on the surface — cushions and lee spots, split currents and eddies, pockets of turbulence and calm — also occur in the vertical plane and the trout are even more likely to take advantage of those as the added dimension of depth means better shelter and camouflage. So pay particular attention to changes in depth — drop-offs, lips, channels and seams — as they are the trout hotspots. Even a single rock is enough to create a holding place for a fish, so let your eyes travel down the edge of a feed line, from rock to rock, and see if any of those have tails.

After you are able to identify the various edges of currents, both on the surface and along the bottom, you begin to stack them up because trout too like to maximise their feeding opportunities. They basically need two things: food and shelter. Food comes down the current lines; shelter is found in depth, and under overhanging vegetation, usually both. Understanding this, putting all the habitat clues together, you're well on your way in developing your 'fish brain', which is an essential attribute of a trout hunter. You ask yourself, 'If I was a fish, where would I be in this piece of water?' then look there. With time and practice you develop an ability to read water as if the trout hideaways were mapped out for you. This is also one of the most satisfying aspects of sight-fishing: to figure out where the fish could be, and then finding them there.

I may be stating the obvious but, in moving water, trout always — ALWAYS — face into the current (to feed and to breathe) and they are streamlined into it so any shape at an odd angle to the flow is unlikely to be a fish. Unless it swims off when you approach, which happens too. One summer day on the Coast, my friend

One of the key skills in successful sight-fishing is the ability to slow down to the pace of water.

and I were staring at a log which almost barred the river and a massive branch protruding upstream from the log, just below the surface. The branch was almost too thick and long to be a trout, but the light was terrible, with drizzly overcast and metallic glare, so we could not tell for sure. We were down on our knees, peering through the clumps of tussock, and the cicadas were too loud to hear ourselves think.

'Have a cast,' Jamie offered.

'Naw, it's not a fish,' I said and stood up.

The 'branch' swam off at speed. It was easily a double-figure fish.

If in doubt, always cast, but fear not, because as you become adept at the trout-spotting game, you'll be spooking a lot of fish too. This is a good thing as, along the way, you can learn not only where they were and how to approach them but what they looked like too. Truth is, with those tough-to-spot trout you rarely see the whole fish clearly. You see hints, visual clues that what you're looking at might just possibly be a fish.

Shape and orientation are primary clues, as are shadows and colour, but what you really want to see is movement. Feeding fish move a lot, side to side when nymphing, or rising in the water column. Sometimes to take an insect close to the bottom the fish will briefly turn side on and you'll see a silvery flash of its flank. Blink and you'll miss it so spend time watching any likely candidate closely, looking for signs of activity. You will still end up casting to sticks, rocks or fish that are resting and will not eat no matter what you throw at them. It's all part of the game. Weeds can be especially deceptive, as some tick all the boxes — right spot, shape, colour, even shadow and, yes, a lot of movement. But like the doggo fish, they don't eat either. It may take you a number of casts and fly changes to figure this out.

One of the key skills in successful sight-fishing is the ability to slow down to the pace of water. There is also a contrary school of thought on this suggesting you should go fast and cover as much water as you can, but I guess you'll only see the obvious fish and you'll spook most and won't even see or know that you have. This was made clear to me one time when I fished on a favourite Southland river with my regular companion, Gore guide Brendan Shields.

On a river, Brendan is as relaxed as they come, nothing to achieve or prove, just the pure contentment of being there. That day his wife Rana was fishing too and as three is an awkward number for sight-fishing I suggested I'd leave them to their nuptial riverside bliss and start way further upstream above them.

'How much water do you need?' I asked Brendan.

'Ah, just leave us a couple of pools.'

We agreed on a landmark and, away from the river, I went upstream above it and fished up from there. I'd put in a decent day, it took over an hour to walk back, and I'd caught half a dozen nice fish and scared off many more. I was feeling perfectly happy with the day and the action, save for a faint twinge of guilt that perhaps I did not leave my friends enough water. I needn't have worried.

'How d'yous go?' I asked back at the camp.

'Really good,' Brendan said, 'hooked nine between here and the corner. Never even got to the second pool.'

On a river, Brendan seems extremely slow, lapsing into long still spaces which to the uninitiated may seem almost comatose, until he says, 'There's one,' pointing the rod tip at the fish most of us would certainly walk past. His strategy takes some getting used to, but it's as relaxing as it is productive.

'You know there are heaps of fish in these Southland rivers. I mean the sheer biomass of trout here is phenomenal,' he says, 'so if you're not seeing fish, it means just that — you're not seeing them, not that they are not there. The slower you go the more you see; you become a part of the trout world, not an intruder into it. And then the river reveals itself to you, it shows you the fish. For me, this searching, anticipating and finding trout is a lot more rewarding than just hauling them in.'

Your eyes are essentially round lenses whose shape is controlled by several pairs of tiny muscles, and good vision is not the matter of their strength but precision, coordination and balance. So, looking for fish, avoid staring hard into the water; it's counterproductive, will fatigue your eyes, lock out your peripheral vision (which is good at picking up movement) and may even give you a headache. Eyes work best when they are continually moving, so let them travel lightly over the water and through it, exploring it as if it was a giant painting. Relaxed, happy eyes will see more than those that try to bore a hole through the water. Look along the bank on your side of the river first; it's amazing how often trout will spook from right under your feet while your eyes are scanning the feed line on the other side.

Ideal spotting conditions would have clear blue sky, strong overhead sun, little or no wind, good high backdrop of trees, cliffs or distant mountains, perhaps some extra elevation to look down from. But of course ideal conditions are rare. In an instructional DVD on how to sight fish in New Zealand, Alberta couple Dave and Amelia Jensen say that, in their experience, about one in four of their fishing days offers conditions which are ideal or close to it. Other times — which is most of the time — we all have to deal with the elements and have strategies to work around them.

Flat overcast light puts an opaque sheen on the river's surface, wind can make it look as if it was frozen, lack of backdrop causes glare and in all these scenarios you will find yourself squinting, staring, tilting your head from side to side, and generally seeing a lot fewer fish. A well-timed hatch can often save a day like that, but otherwise you need to make the most of sighting opportunities that you do have. Go slower — the fish can see you much better in the overcast as there is a lot less contrast between below and above and they are not looking into the sun. Remember, it's one top predator hunting another and, with the odds in the trout's favour, you really need to lift your game just to stay in it.

Seek any elevation you can find, any backdrop to look against, even if you're looking down the river. When you are moving slowly and stealthily, as a hunter should, it's not uncommon to see a fish downstream of yourself, backtrack quietly and still get an opportunity to cast to it. In tough light is also where having best-quality glasses becomes critical. Skimp on other gear when you must but, if you're serious about sight-fishing, you need the best polarised glasses you can afford.

Dean Bell has been considered 'one of the best if not the best trout guide in New Zealand', and though such accolades are highly subjective and impossible to ascertain, one sure thing I can tell you about him is that he has the best eyes of anyone I've ever fished with. Years ago, we were on a Fiordland river together and I still remember being absolutely astonished by the acuity of his eyesight. We fished in fast broken water, single nymphs with no indicators, and while I — back then a serious sight-fishing rookie — struggled to make out the fish themselves, Dean could see, and call, the takes, and — you know what? — never once did he make a dud call.

'My Polaroid glasses are the most important piece of fishing equipment I own,' Dean says, 'and when your reputation as a guide is on the line every day you cannot afford to use anything but the best.' Although there is a plethora of brands on the market, from cheap and nasty disposables to chic designer frames, Dean, and many other guides who fish mainly with their eyes, letting the clients do the rest of the work, tend to almost unanimously favour the Smith optics.

'They really stand apart as a brand because the quality of their glass; its contrast, filtering and optical precision are unmatched,' Dean says. 'This allows me to find trout everybody else has walked past . . . what some might call "the impossible trout to see". Plus, Smith continually develop their technology, as evident with the low-light Ignitor lenses. The Ignitors especially are without compare. They allow in forty per cent more light while still polarising it. Kind of makes an overcast day sunny again.'

The first time I used the low-light Ignitor lenses on a dark dull Southland day I remember thinking to myself, 'Man, I can see! I can see again!' They are a little too light for full sun so, of course, you'll need another darker pair for those perfect days. The enduring joy of fly-fishing is that you can always buy more stuff. But, as you're parting with your hard-earned cash, keep in mind this time you are not buying gadgets but the most essential tool in your fishing kit. Why? Because, as one smart-arse commented: 'in sight fishing, if you can't see the fish or your fly, you don't really need a fly rod'.

In the end, when you have put in plenty of riverside mileage, spooked enough fish and learnt from that, when you've learnt to read the water and pick out its clues, seeing trout becomes almost a sixth sense. You can't even explain how or why, but you know that the shape you're looking at is a fish, even if your companion may suspect you are hallucinating. At times, you'll still cast to rocks and sticks, and weeds especially, though less and less so. There is a particular softness and fluid grace to the shape of trout, which other river features do not have, and you learn to recognise it. It'll draw your eyes in as if by magic.

How do you know you're there? When you start doubting yourself, when what your mind dismissed as 'not a fish' swims off at speed just as you take another step. So, when in doubt, always cast. Some rocks and weeds I've seen have been known to even come up to the surface and take a dry and put up a good fight afterwards too.

Be forewarned, though, fly-fishing at this level is addictive in its intensity. It redefines both skills and expectations, and the way you want to engage with trout. It's like developing a taste for single malts — after you've done so, it's no longer satisfying to go back to the cheap stuff. Equally, I now find it less than thrilling to mindlessly flog water blind, hoping for something to happen, though I have to say, since I've discovered Spey casting, this too is beginning to change. Maybe the poetry of the cast itself has added a new dimension to the game, substituting for the act of hunting, and I now again enjoy fishing, and catching fish, without seeing them first. It also happens that Spey is one of Jennifer's favourite ways to fish. I'll tell you more about it later in this narrative.

At the Southern Lakes the spring runs of spawning rainbows was in full swing, the season had only just opened and most of the streams feeding into the lakes were full of fish. This is about as easy as fly-fishing gets in New Zealand and though there are local purists who would scoff at 'stupid rainbows' that will take 'anything you throw at them', for me this event is one of the highlights of the trout year, a rare opportunity to experience fish which have pretty much never seen a human.

I distinctly remember catching one of those fish three times! I saw him nymphing voraciously on the lip of a drop-off. I hooked him on the first cast and he tore off down the creek, jumping and bouncing off the surface like a basketball. A few metres below me he came off the hook and I watched him come back up, and on his way he took a couple of nymphs as they drifted by, his flank flashing silver no more than three or four metres above me. Then he was back on the drop-off, feeding as if nothing ever happened, and I cast and caught him again, and the same thing happened, only this time he came off on one of his aerials. And still he came back up and resumed feeding. I checked the fly and saw that the hook was bent open and so I changed it and caught the fish again, this time netting him after a solid fight.

The fish clearly did not associate the two previous hook-ups and fights with anything out of the ordinary or he would have spooked or at least stopped feeding. It makes you wonder what the fish would behave like in the total absence of predators such as anglers and just how much and how quickly they learn from being caught and released, and from having repeated human encounters.

With all this in mind, I usually limit myself to just one day on each of the creeks — maybe two or three days of this *rainbow indulgence* in total — further ramping up the challenge by using my 3-wt rod, single barbless flies and no indicators, and insisting on first seeing every single fish I cast to.

The trout average around three pounds, which is plenty big in small intimate water, and they are eager and aggressive to a point of stealing flies in front of each other, and you get to see a lot of them, and have plenty of shots, which is why I thought Jennifer's progression into New Zealand fly-fishing could benefit greatly from it. After all, there is nothing better for healing a bruised ego and restoring your confidence than catching a dozen or more good fish in a day and making yourself feel like a champ again. Or so you'd think . . .

We started up one of the creeks and there were fish everywhere. I mean, it was hard to decide which one to cast to. And still she fumbled, and tangled, and hooked up trees behind us, and piled up her line on top of fish. It all soon became frustrating in the extreme: me catching one fish after another with precise single casts, Jennifer not being able to get her fly near a trout. She was close to tears, and maybe she cried when I wasn't watching. My spirits had sunk too, and a persistently sad thought kept echoing in my mind: 'If you can't catch a fish here then our entire trout dream safari is in danger of disintegrating. It's just not going to work like this.'

With nothing more to say or suggest, I did the only thing I could think of: I left her a riffle stacked with trout and went downstream to give each of us some space and time out. A hundred metres below, I saw a couple of fish against the opposite bank and found momentary delight in plopping my nymph a hand-length from the bank and its overhanging grasses, with just the right

After all, there is nothing better for healing a bruised ego and restoring your confidence than catching a dozen or more good fish in a day . . .

amount of upstream reach mend, and I got them both, all the while thinking it would have been so much better if Jennifer caught them, not me.

Just then, I looked upstream, simultaneously hearing her telltale scream, and I saw a good fish in full spawning colours cartwheeling above the water. But even before I could applaud and rush in with the net, there was another scream, short and exasperated, and I knew the fish was gone.

Jen waved at me, happy again, and resumed fishing and I saw that her loops were clean and her line straight and so it was only a few more casts before she hooked up again, and this time we netted the fish, a magnificently coloured rainbow that looked like a flame streaking through the water.

Now that I was near her I pointed out another fish and Jen cast to it, but it was no good. She hooked up on a branch above the trout – well above it – and lost the fly. When I retied it, she hung up the first backcast.

I left her alone and she caught that fish, and another, then several others. There was a pattern emerging here.

At the end of the day, Jennifer had caught several good fish – each of which would have been a trophy in Colorado – and she did it all without my help; in fact precisely because I did not help.

'You have graduated,' I said, enveloping her in a hug at our turnaround point. 'The preschool is over!'

She pulled away, slapping me on the shoulder, but she was laughing. We both were.

It was clear that to begin with we were trying too hard and it wasn't fun. We were both putting too much pressure on ourselves: I badly wanted her to catch fish; she wanted to show me that she could. Put together, this did not work particularly well. But the alternative — of each of us fishing alone — wasn't an option either. This was not why we came together and what we dreamed about.

'Somehow, you need to get over this paralysis that comes over you when I'm standing nearby and pointing out the trout,' I said. 'Otherwise it'll be impossible for us to fish together.'

'I'm trying! I'm trying really hard. Maybe too hard.'

It took some doing. I broke my own rule — exceptional circumstances, you understand — and we went back to the same creek twice more. By the end of that, Jennifer had caught more fish than she'd care to count. She had even started to spot fish for me and laugh at my own goof-ups.

Finally it all came together, a couple of weeks later, on a river with a distant view of Aoraki/Mt Cook. For the first time ever, we were no longer the guide and the guided, an 'expert' and a rookie, but just two friends fishing together regardless of skills and outcomes, taking turns fish for fish, spotting and watching the trout for each other, happy and relaxed. Well, at least as relaxed as you can get seeing four-and five-pound trout taking dry flies with audible slurps.

We were learning about each other and it was work in progress. Good progress.

'I'll fish with you anytime, anywhere,' I said.

And she told me:

'I wouldn't want it any other way. It's the happiest I've ever been.'

chapter 2

LAST TIME I CAME TO FISH in Golden Bay, some years ago, a long-time friend invited me to a barbecue. He stressed I needn't bring anything as he had just caught a fish and it was big enough to feed us all. I saw the fish wrapped in aluminium foil and it was huge. I knew that Martin had just got into fishing for salmon, and had made a trip or two to the mouth of the Hurunui, and so I fully assumed the fish was a chinook caught at the river mouth and brought home to the Bay. But no, Martin corrected me, it was a brown trout, caught in a local river, just a few minutes from his place. He went out for a 'flick' with his spinning rod one night and on a third or fourth cast hooked and landed the monster that was now feeding close to a dozen people.

I daren't even try to guess the size of that brown, but, as I said, I thought it was a good-size salmon. I've caught some large trout in my years, a few double-figure ones, but nothing remotely close to what we ate that night. And so GB, as it is locally known, has long held a particular attraction for me, for this and other reasons, and I wanted to revisit it and now to also show Jennifer this unique part of New Zealand.

Golden Bay, of course, encompasses the northern parts of Kahurangi National Park, which is renowned for its large brown trout. It is also a relatively remote end-of-the-road kind of place where organic hippies, artists and New Agers blend harmoniously with salt-of-the-earth farmers, a green sunny enclave where life seems to still go on at a pleasantly relaxed pace and where, may this never change, there are still more yoga teachers than cops.

We set up a base at Collingwood motorcamp, on a treed peninsula where the Aorere River — the largest in the Bay — enters the estuary. The following morning, the only resident GB fishing guide, Anton Donaldson, came to pick us up and the plan was to fish together on one of the smaller local streams, one that we did not know at all and which Anton visited only infrequently. I find it is always better to fish with guides as buddies than being guided by them; the quality of experience is similar but the atmosphere a lot more relaxed. The day was perfectly sunny, still and full of promise and we took an instant liking to Anton. I told him the story of Martin's monster fish and hinted that perhaps we could visit the very creek where he caught it.

But Anton, though an easy-going and cheerful fellow, was not optimistic about the prospects, much less the outcomes. We

We could certainly go exploring but finding trout . . . errr . . . that could be problematic. Haven't I been following the news, he asked. Golden Bay was regularly making national headlines and not for very happy reasons.

could certainly go exploring but finding trout . . . errr . . . that could be problematic. Haven't I been following the news, he asked. Golden Bay was regularly making national headlines and not for very happy reasons.

Over recent years, the area had been hit by a string of floods of uncommon severity, Anton said. In 2009, there was a once in twenty-five-year flood, when 300 millimetres of rain fell in twenty-four hours and the Takaka River, usually flowing at twenty cubic metres per second, peaked at 1500. The following December, a once-in-150-year flood hit and the Aorere River raged at 3500 cumecs. Then, in 2011, 674 millimetres of rain fell on the Bay in forty-eight hours, an unprecedented deluge which damaged homes, roads and bridges. There was another cloudburst in February 2016, with 528 millimetres of rain recorded in forty-eight hours, but by then the never-before-seen weather extremes were becoming the new normal.

What was not in the news and eye-catching weather stats was that the cumulative effect of those floods had more or less obliterated the local trout fishery. Farmers reported finding dead fish in the paddocks once the flood waters receded, and for the first time since the introduction of trout in the 1860s Fish & Game began restocking the rivers to help the trout come back from the brink of local extinction.

Anton still lived in the Bay, and loved it, but now he did most of his fishing, and guiding, outside the Bay, often going as far as Murchison and the West Coast.

'Fish & Game did a drift dive down the Takaka River and they found seven trout,' he said, and I thought, 'I've caught more than that in a day there and that without walking very far.'

We walked some ten river kilometres that day, along well-structured banks and pockets of good holding water. Jennifer would later say it was one of the prettiest places she'd ever fished. But we never saw a single trout.

There was a gorge at the top of the beat, where the river came out of the mountains, and Anton assured us there were always a few trout there. This was to be our redemption as those fish rarely saw an angler. I liked his confidence, but when we finally came across those fish they were skittish and obviously spooked, and we never got even a single cast to any of them.

On the way back, we came across a tiny backcountry hut which, Jennifer suggested, we should immediately buy and move into. Inside there was a visitors' book.

'Look!' Anton exclaimed, opening it to the current page. 'I can't believe this!'

In the book, a short entry for this same day detailed how a local angler had hiked into the gorge and caught himself a nice fish, and lost another, while his wife went botanising in the forest. The oddest thing was, it was the first entry this season, which had been open for nearly six weeks by now. Several previous entries were months old and they were made by hunters and hikers, not anglers.

'That's just plain bad luck,' Anton shrugged, and there was no arguing with that.

That night, back at the campground, we too got to experience the new vagaries of the Golden Bay weather. A storm came through from the sea and it hit the land as if it tried to level it. We were camped in the stand of old pines, nosed into the wind on the edge of a breakwater several metres high above the river and the estuary. Horizontal rain pelted against the canopy and all night the camper rocked on its suspension like a boxer dodging an endless barrage of punches.

We did not get much sleep.

'Should we move?' Jennifer kept asking as the gusts of wind picked up river water from below and threw it against the windscreen.

'I think we're fine,' I kept saying, each time less sure.

'Been here for years, never seen anything like it,' Gary, the camp custodian, muttered in the morning as he surveyed the damage.

There were heaps of debris and flotsam piled up where the night before people were drinking wine and watching the sunset, . . .

While protected by the trees in our corner of the camp we weathered the storm unscathed, if a little groggy from the lack of sleep, the other side of the camp, exposed both to the wind and the sea, was trashed and abandoned.

It turned out that Gary spent most of his night evacuating campers from their seaside spots, towing them off to safe ground with his quad bike while volumes of seawater poured out from the interiors and the engine compartments. There were heaps of debris and flotsam piled up where the night before people were drinking wine and watching the sunset, and the river below the breakwater wall ran brown and foamy and several times the size it was the night before.

'There won't be any trout fishing in the Bay for at least a couple of days,' Anton told us when he came visiting in the morning, to see how we had fared, 'but you can always have a look at the flats. They are protected from the nor'west storms by Farewell Spit so they should be about as clear as they get.'

Unless you live and fish on the moon, you'd have by now surely heard or read about the Golden Bay kingfish which come into knee-deep water to feed on palm-size baitfish, and which can be stalked and sight-fished just like trout, only a lot bigger and endowed with incomparably more horsepower. Well, it was Anton Donaldson who discovered the fishery. One day a few years back, he was fishing for food out in the Bay from his twelve-foot boat when the sea turned rough and forced him to seek shelter closer inshore. Some fifty metres from the beach, and in shallow water now, he ran over a stingray, a large black diamond with undulating sides, ghosting over yellow-white sand. Riding on top of and slightly behind the stingray, like jet fighters accompanying a

'It almost certainly appears that the kingfish are using the stingrays as an ambush vehicle,' Anton said. 'They seem to be able to get closer to the baitfish schools when they "ride" the stingrays . . .

bomber, were two large fish which Anton instantly recognised as yellowtail kingfish.

'I continued towards Collingwood and again I saw a ray with another set of kingfish in tow,' he recalled.

The following day he returned with a softbait rod and caught a few kingfish, then he came back again with an 8-wt fly rod and large trout streamers. These worked even better and so the softbait would stay home from then on.

Though with more time spent on the flats Anton would start seeing the kingfish tailing and target those too, the black stingrays remained the main clue in the hunt.

'It almost certainly appears that the kingfish are using the stingrays as an ambush vehicle,' Anton said. 'They seem to be able to get closer to the baitfish schools when they "ride" the stingrays, which gives them a head start in chasing down their meal.'

Kingfish vary in size from around 650 millimetres to over a metre long, but they can be tough to see, especially on an overcast day, as they move fast and blend perfectly with the sand. But stingrays — slower, a metre across, and the only black thing in the pastel wash of aquamarines and tawny whites — attract the eye from a couple of hundred metres away.

'Find a ray and you'll find kingfish,' Anton said, 'and maybe kahawai [Australian salmon] as well, as they come in to feed on baitfish too. Then, you just run like hell through knee-to-waist-deep water to intercept the ray so you can cast ahead of it.'

He gave us the right flies and told us where to go.

'In saltwater fly-fishing there are long periods of nothing

happening interspersed with bursts of frantic action, so be patient,' he said as a farewell. 'It can be great, or it can be humbling. On a good day, you can get thirty to forty shots, on other days you'd swear there are no kingfish in the whole of Golden Bay. It's a little early in the season, but you never know. Best days of your lives might be waiting for you on the saltwater flats.'

Of that I was certain, especially because it was Jennifer's turn to be the guide. She's had considerable saltwater experience — on Christmas Island, Florida and Mexico — and she loved it.

'In salt, it's fly-fishing stripped down to the most basic and pure: one fly, wading barefoot on the sand, just the ocean and you looking for fish, not even casting until you see something,' she told me.

For me this was going to be the first real venture into saltwater fly-fishing. I say first 'real' because I discount one previous attempt when, more than a decade ago, I was invited to write about the first New Zealand saltwater fly-fishing 'championships' organised by an Auckland outfitter, which sadly turned out to involve chumming up the water off the back of two boats and casting into the feeding frenzy that resulted, sometimes catching a fish, other times a seagull. I was so appalled by this bloodbath I refused to write the assigned story, and the overall experience put a serious damper on my trying to fly-fish in salt water again.

But this hunting of kingfish over knee-deep flats had all the elements of our art that I find appealing: sighting of the quarry first and the need for accurate casting, the need to observe and figure out a whole new set of clues and conditions, a steep learning curve that precluded any notions of instant gratification but instead made you work hard for the rewards, thus making them all the more valuable. It was fair on the fish and challenging to an angler and, hell, I'd be guided by a girl, possibly *my* girl.

Besides, though a complete rookie at this style of fly-fishing I had long-felt nostalgia for the Bay's salt water, a memory of some other 'best days of my life'. Many years ago — too many to admit the exact figure — I worked as a professional diver in Golden Bay. We were harvesting a species of clam called geoduck, a bivalve mollusc which lives in the underwater sand of the Bay and whose siphon looks like, well, that distinctive part of the male anatomy, on steroids. Geoducks were going to be the next big thing in seafood, with the Asian markets poised with their chopsticks ready and awaiting shipments, and we felt like being a part of a new gold rush, earning a good living while indulging in an adventure.

Like black neons, pulsating against yellow-white background, they were coming in, one after another, along a tidal channel which we soon nicknamed Stingray Alley . . .

We would steam out at 4.30 a.m. from Pohara Wharf, and the entire Bay would be glass-out still. Dolphins would come out and play in our bow wave, guiding us out, and looking back towards the land, we could see the snow still crowning the tops of the Arthur, Anatoki and Waingaro ranges which so well isolate the Bay from the rest of the world. All in all, it was a vision of Paradise, if I ever saw one.

Our gold rush eventually fizzled out, as they all do, though the memories of those diving days are still as vivid as they were when we lived them. The oddest thing is — though we spent up to five or six hours a day under water — except for the geoducks, horse mussels and an odd octopus I remembered the water as being completely devoid of fish life. I guess with the compressors, water-jet hoses and all the noise we made we would have scared off everything within a wide radius of the mother ship.

This time, wading hand in hand on to the kingfish flats, we were a definition of stealth — slow and quiet and fishing only with our eyes. 'Everything else is moving in the ocean so you see a lot more when you're still,' Jennifer said, her eyes scanning the horizon. The tide was only just starting to creep in and in ankle-deep warm water there were entire shoals of finger-length baitfish, swimming and turning in unison, casting wiggly black shadows over light sand.

We had to wade out several hundred metres before the water was deep enough to fish. After you've spent years training your eyes to see the shadowy clues of camouflaging trout, the stingrays on the flats are not exactly hard to see. Like black neons, pulsating against yellow-white background, they were coming in, one after another, along a tidal channel which we soon nicknamed Stingray Alley, majestically flying under water, only inches off the bottom.

'They are here!' I heard Jennifer shout. 'A whole bunch of big fish has just shot past me!'

'Are they kingfish?' I yelled back, but in the excitement of the moment, with her hood done up tight against a stiff breeze, she did not hear me.

From her rod keeper she unhooked a fly the size of a small bird and began casting like a woman possessed.

We fished the flats for three days solid, cast to dozens of rays, changed flies and tides, and we never even saw a kingfish, much less hooked one. The fish that had so excited Jennifer turned out to be a group of kahawai, and they passed through quickly, not to be seen again. The cold snap that followed the storm which upturned the Collingwood camp had chilled the air and the water, and it was too cold to wade the flats for more than couple of hours at a time. The southerly coming down the mountains was brutal and frigid, and it made the white dunes of the distant Farewell Spit smoke with billowing sand like a string of low volcanoes. There were no kingfish riding the rays. Not yet.

'You're about a month too early,' Anton concluded when I updated him about our lack of progress. 'I thought it'd be worth a try, but if the fish are not there you can't catch them. Come back after Christmas, when the sea has warmed up properly.'

We would, but not this year. What we fished was the only time slot we had here; by Christmas we'd be in Colorado and Jen would be showing me her mountains and her home rivers.

At the camp, Gary offered some sympathy but also a solution. 'Why don't you borrow my surfcasters and fish the river mouth?' he suggested. 'Get some frozen bait at the store here, you'll be sure to catch something.'

I thanked him for being helpful and oh so practical but did not have the heart to explain that, if you take up a high challenge, like sight-fishing to fast-moving pelagics, you have to learn the ropes and pay your dues, that in this kind of game blank days are as inevitable as they are educational, and that, as hard as this might be to believe, for us *how* we caught fish was fundamentally more important that *what* we caught or *if*.

Still, after a fishless hike in the backcountry and now three blank days on the flats, Jennifer was getting increasingly antsy.

'Man, I need to catch something and soon,' she said.

'I thought you didn't care if you caught fish or not,' I teased her.

'Well, ye-ah! Usually, I don't. But I haven't had a fish on for days now and I'm starting to forget what it feels like.'

I pondered our options: we both loved the Bay—Jen had fallen in love with it the day we arrived in Collingwood—but the fishing was terrible so maybe it was time to move. It turned out, Golden Bay had one more surprise in store for us, as good as it was unexpected.

'On our way out let's try the Cobb River,' I suggested. It was a gamble—a long torturous drive into the alpine hydro lake and river that feeds it—but I had caught some large brown trout there in the past so there was hope for more and, besides, the place was scenic enough for a romantic and remote camp spot if nothing else.

I had no idea there was a run of rainbow trout up the Cobb; after all, Kahurangi was brown trout country. But because of the large hydro reservoir a good population of rainbows has been established there and they have their annual late-spring spawning run just like the rainbows in the Southern Lakes, and we just so happened to arrive at its peak.

As we started up the river the following morning there were fish everywhere. The only three or four browns we saw skulked away without ever giving us a clean chance but the rainbows—small though pretty and spirited—took our nymphs as if they had never seen an artificial fly. The forest and the valley soon echoed with Jennifer's girly screams and high on the trail above the river, hikers would stop in their strides and look down searching for the source of these noises, wondering perhaps just what we were up to down there to be having so much fun.

The fishing was about as easy as it can get, though, after the lull of the previous few days, it was good to feel that familiar electricity surging up the line and through the rod tip, between the fish and our hands, and hearts. In the end, having lost count of fish several times over, even Jennifer had reached her fill.

'Okay mister, enough of this child's play,' she said. 'I am ready for a big bad brown trout, or a few.'

And so we headed down the West Coast, to engage in a 'disappearing act' I had so long been promising her.

chapter 3

IN THE REEFTON BACKCOUNTRY, we were three nymph changes into the game: Jennifer thigh-deep in the impossibly clear water of another emerald pool, laying quiet casts along the current seam, me high up on the rocks of the opposite bank, camouflaged against them, watching a trophy trout ignoring her flies. We were keeping the game pure and fair, as we usually do — single nymphs and no indicators — and the fish was still happy and undisturbed, feeding with abandon that is a joy to see. It sat in a vein of current formed by two big rocks, in water that was fast and riffled and probably a lot deeper than it looked.

'Maybe you're not getting deep enough,' I offered. 'Put on something heavier.'

'Got just the fly for it, a Two-Bit Hooker,' Jen said, tying it on. 'Watch this!'

For her the fish was in the glare, but from my perfect vantage point I saw the nymph plopping some five feet ahead of it, and I saw the huge trout swing to the side, an unmistakable sign it has taken something.

'Yep! You're ON!' I yelled.

She stumbled back on the strike but steadied herself and the battle began.

'Oh my gawd! Oh my gawd! I can't hold him!'

Each of the trout's blistering runs was accompanied by Jen's girly scream, increasing in pitch until the fish stopped. This strategy seemed to work well, though she also used good side pressure, forcing the fish to work hard against the current and the rod.

'Just calm him down now, we're almost there,' I called, slithering from my rock and into the water, net in hand.

I was halfway across the current when I heard a sickening ping and Jen's line snapped out of the water as if in a backcast.

'Noooooo!' her cry echoed off the walls of the gorge.

And a few moments later: 'What did I do wrong?'

I ran the leader through my fingers.

'You did nothing wrong,' I said. 'Look!'

The nymph was still on and the knots were solid, but the hook was bent open, almost straight.

What do you tell someone who's just lost the trout of a lifetime? I held her until she stopped quivering, then said, 'Don't worry luv, we'll find you another big fish.'

And we did, just around the next corner.

There was no shortage of good trout in this remote backcountry river but we worked for them hard. We four-wheel drove up a long forest track, rode further in on our mountain bikes, tramped on some more, and only then we broke out our fishing gear. It'd been days since we saw another angler, another human being for that matter. I won't bore you with the blow-by-blow account of our fishing prowess or the lack of it. Suffice to say trout was only one of the reasons we were here. It was all a part of a larger and carefully crafted plan, what I've come to call 'the disappearing act'.

I first discovered fly-fishing as a cure-all for the world's problems a couple of days after 9/11 when, faced with such a monumental display of human insanity, about all I could do was to go to the river. The spring run of rainbows was at its peak in the Southern Lakes, the water was snow-cold, the fish plentiful and easy to intercept at the river mouth, and so I deemed the therapy a success pretty much from day one.

Later I realised that the effects of this panacea can be multiplied by going remote, ideally out of cell and Wi-Fi range, away from the news and social media, and for several days at a time. Somehow, the river world of bugs and trout has come to be more real and true to me than a lot that's going on in our human society: the theatrical farce of daily politics, the warmongering, the incessant noise of mainstream media and the overload of meaningless information and celebrity gossip, the 'rockstar economy' so blinded by short-term profits it totally disregards the harm it's doing to the very planet and its ecosystems that sustain us. So, you can imagine, considering the state of the world's affairs, I've been fishing a lot, though probably nowhere near enough.

Not that my fishing actually solved any of the world's problems, but then nothing else I could do would achieve that anyway. What it did do was to shift my attention from what I could worry about or fear to what I love and that was good enough for me. Your priorities change when in the woods by the river: to find feeding fish and try to catch them, have a level camp and enough firewood for the evening, enough food, fuel and firewater, being in companionable silence with yourself and any friends you've brought along, trying not to over-talk it all, and let the river and the woods do the talking instead.

There is ample scientific and medical evidence that, biologically at least, we are still hunters and gatherers, built to move and roam, to live outside, to get hot and cold, dead tired and then well rested, hungry and full . . .

There is ample scientific and medical evidence that, biologically at least, we are still hunters and gatherers, built to move and roam, to live outside, to get hot and cold, dead tired and then well rested, hungry and full, to feel the uneven earth beneath our feet, sunlight on our skin and, I like to think, the river currents against our legs. We have not evolved to live in concrete jungles, swipe touch screens and watch bad television, to spend our lives in closed air-conned spaces under fluorescent lights, eating food that is hard to distinguish from its packaging and taking health supplements for what is freely available outside. (The game-changing book on this subject is *Younger Next Year* by Chris Crowley which I cannot recommend enough, especially to anyone over fifty.)

So, in a way, a *disappearing act* is a — albeit brief — return to who we really are, or at least supposed to be. It is not running away to hide from the world but going to the source to recharge so that you can come back stronger and deal with things better. And, besides, fishing — as in catch-and-release fly-fishing in remote places — may seem totally meaningless to an outsider, but as the inimitable Robert Traver told us, 'I fish [. . .] not because I regard fishing as being so terribly important, but because I suspect that so many of the other concerns of men are equally unimportant and not nearly so much fun.'

Come to think of it, a disappearing act does not need to be a multi-day backcountry epic either. Many of my most memorable ones have been 4WD camping trips, and my Landcruiser camper has been a perfect mobile basecamp for these ever since I got it over a decade ago. Even with only a little bit of topo research there is untold potential for such adventures in New Zealand.

'I'm constantly amazed by the perceived wildness and remoteness of the places you take me to fish in this country,' Jennifer told me as we sat by a campfire on an empty beach, the only visible lights those of a distant lighthouse, a fishing boat on the horizon and the stars getting ever brighter with the nightfall. We had just fished all day, and would fish another river tomorrow, but we camped on the beach because of the abundance of firewood and to get away from the sandflies.

'If this was America, there would be condos and "No Trespassing" signs everywhere,' Jen went on. 'Into any place that has decent fishing, the gazillionaires move in and they buy up huge swathes of land, privatise the access and effectively make the land disappear to everyone but themselves. It's a different kind of disappearing act. You don't really know how fortunate you are here.'

And I thought, maybe some of us do. Considering that foreign anglers are prepared to pay upwards of $1000 a day to disappear on New Zealand trout rivers, and taking into account just how many such days I had for myself over the past three decades, and if that's what they are truly worth in financial terms, I'm something of a gazillionaire myself, in experiences anyway, if not quite on the bank statement.

Whether you tramp into the wild for days or road-trip in a 4x4, a disappearing act needs certain key ingredients to do what it's supposed to do. It has to be a full immersion in the trout world, not a dabble between returns to the lodge, pub and cell reception. You have your coffee with the sunrise and your single malt, or whatever you drink, at sundown, and you tune into the cycles of insects and fish, the periods of activities and the times of rest. If you can, you forget what day of the week it is, you wash with the river water and dry off in the sun and the wind. You unplug from the noise of society — don't worry, it'll be there when you come out — and you listen to and explore both outer and inner silences, you turn off all your devices and let the river be your music.

It helps if you can disappear with one of your best friends, too, even if that means yourself only. For a decade and a half I've fished with my dogs and they'd both been stellar river companions, always happy and eager — Maya even learnt to point rising fish for me — though in this country fishing with dogs entails so many limitations it's always something of a compromise just how and where you can go with them.

Choosing a human fishing companion to disappear with is a whole other subject. They can either ruin your experience or enhance and magnify it beyond measure, and if you read my *Trout Bohemia* you'll know just what level of companionship I did aspire to. Mysteriously and miraculously, this was now materialising before my eyes with the arrival of Jennifer who seemed to not only share my passion for the world of trout but also my attitudes towards it. Maybe dreams — trout or otherwise — do come true, and so together we hope to take the disappearing act to a whole new order of magnitude, where being with the rivers is our preferred new normal and coming back to 'reality' a necessary aberration.

But don't get too hung up on the prerequisites and preferences. Go and do it! Allow yourself the gift of doing a disappearing act, even if only for a weekend. Don't fret about the details, they'll work themselves out. You forget to pack sugar, you'll drink your coffee without it. Life is really a lot simpler out there. The most important thing is to make a start at this unorthodox way of saving the world.

You see, the kid in the *Into the Wild* movie and book may have been naive and incompetent in the bush — maybe if he had a fly rod he would have fed himself better — but his ideas and ideals were pure and true. We have become so disconnected from our natural world, our natural state, we have forgotten who we are and what our place is in the great scheme of Life. To the point that something called nature deficit disorder has become a recognised medical condition, affecting mainly children, though, considering our lifestyles and the increasingly artificial and polluted environments, none of us is totally immune from it.

I often have to tell my clients that, coming from their hyperactive daily life and overachiever work routines into fly-fishing for trout, they need to slow down to the pace of the water they fish. One guy took all of four days. He was impatient, brusque and so wired I wondered if he seriously OD'd on caffeine every morning before we even met. He just wanted to 'get things done' on the river as he would at work. Alas, trout are not on anyone's schedule, except their own, and they respond predictably to an agitated approach and so they humbled the guy to a state where he stopped believing he'd ever catch anything. I nearly gave up on him too, but then there was a good hatch of mayflies and I left him to it with a couple of matched flies and suggestions how to use them, and all on his own he caught a fish, then another, then a couple more, and when

As a popular saying goes, 'There is no Wi-Fi out there in the woods but the connection is a lot better.'

the hatch was over he came back to me beaming so happily I feared he was about to give me a hug.

'You know, I've just come off this long and incredibly stressful contract,' he told me, 'today is the first day in weeks I've been able to relax.'

He fished well for the rest of the week, a changed man. Trout waters have such powers of returning us to an equilibrium, washing away the mental garbage our minds are so quick to produce and store, energising our bodies and spirits, bringing us back to true priorities and the simplicity that is a key ingredient of contentment.

Thus my *disappearing act* is a way of going back to who we are, a start in undoing the damage of having lost our natural ways. As a popular saying goes, 'There is no Wi-Fi out there in the woods but the connection is a lot better.'

We just happen to go there with a fly rod.

By now, it was early summer. We were road-tripping down the West Coast of the South Island, the land of glacial rivers and hidden spring creeks, and wherever we found good trout water, happy fish were rising to dry flies, the dimples in the water spreading out as if the rivers themselves were smiling at us. Jennifer seemed to exist in a state of perpetual wonder and ecstatic daze, like a child checking again and again for the presents under the Christmas tree and every time finding something new and exciting, and I could not help but to bask in this joy and enthusiasm that were as palpable as sunshine.

Guiding — and especially too much guiding — no matter how well-intentioned and executed, carries with it an inherent danger of the guides becoming cynical about the very thing we love because so often (though with notable exceptions) we have to deal with huge expectations and little or no skills to match them. Jennifer, to the contrary, had no expectations at all, and she was happy with whatever the days brought — hatch or no hatch, plenty of fish or none. Her skills were slowly consolidating to meet the higher challenges and she was eager to learn, though for her, it wasn't really about trying to understand it all, more about just having enough information to better enjoy her encounters with the trout.

Her entire approach to fly-fishing, with nothing to prove but the whole world of trout to be lived, experienced and appreciated, was so fresh and pure it could melt any residual cynicism in the most hard-nosed guide, the way the aforementioned sunshine would dissolve and evaporate any ice it fell upon. Just being with her on a river made me see everything there anew again, an odd but precious sensation after thirty years on the water.

The fishing, too, was as good as it gets: honest, visual, intense and oh so rewarding, especially since we more or less disposed of our nymph boxes for the rest of summer. Yes, you'll no doubt read elsewhere that something like ninety per cent of trout food are nymphs and that you'll catch more fish on nymphs than on anything else. Equally true was that, by now, Jennifer and I were happy to target the remaining ten per cent.

There is perhaps no sight more dear to the eyes and hearts of fly anglers than the nose of a trout breaking the fluid surface of the water, rising to intercept an insect or, if we are fortunate and skilled enough, our artificial imitation of it.

Beetles and blowflies, mayflies, caddis, damsels and willow grubs, hoppers and cicadas — the hallmarks of New Zealand trout summer — each elicit subtly and not-so-subtly different takes, and distinguishing among them can be a science in itself. Often you can make the distinctions by the sound alone: willow grub take is like a wet kiss while a cicada one is more like a punch through the surface. Mayfly rises — to floating nymphs, emergers, duns or spents — are the hardest of all to tell apart while caddis takes are unmistakably splashy. But whatever the insects on the surface of the water, they can often drive trout into a frenzy of excitement and as if by resonance we respond in the same way. For one, I'm absolutely sure that the fact trout rise to dry fly, with such aggression, curiosity and confidence, is the very reason I fish for them.

After a winter of shooting-head lines and streamers, and the early-season weeks of lobbing out heavy tungsten nymphs, casting a summer dry fly is a joy, regardless of its kind or size. But rookie anglers beware! Decent casting and good patterns are only a part of the dry-fly game. By far the most important though often overlooked factor is that whatever fly you use, it must float through the trout's field of vision naturally and without drag.

And I don't mean the drag on your reel! The dragging of a fly is caused by the current pulling on your fly line, often in different directions along its length, which in turn makes the fly move in a way and with speed no natural insect would or could do. Dragging a fly over a happily feeding fish is one sure way to spook it. It is also one of the main causes for refusals. You'd often see anglers frantically changing flies, one after another, hoping to find the magic pattern that'd work and catch that rising fish, while all along the reason for the fish not taking is not the choice of the fly but the way we present it.

Over the years of fly-fishing I have become something of a dry-fly purist, not through snobbery of any kind but because of simple aesthetic preferences, reinforced perhaps by similar attitudes of people I tend to fish with. Now, I was thrilled to find that, of all styles and species — tarpon, bonefish, permit and steelhead included —Jennifer loved dry-fly fishing for trout most of all. Only that to tune to New Zealand realities she needed to lift her game a couple of notches.

It turned out that most of the rivers she regularly fished in Colorado were predominately riffly, often with long stretches bordering on whitewater and, with some 6000 fish per mile, the quality of presentations was almost never critical. Which was about the extreme opposite of the West Coast spring creeks. Here, one sloppy cast, one drag of the fly over the trout, one mistimed mend and it was 'Okay, let's go and find another fish for you.' And so, in casting sessions in our camps, then in real-life application on the rivers and creeks we fished the following days, we set out to straighten a few things in her presentations, to take the kinks out of it as it were, then to put them back in, only this time on purpose.

When you learn to cast, and even during the intermediate phase of your fly-fishing progression, you want to be casting a straight line as this is the entry point to the kind of accuracy required to fool New Zealand trout. But as you move up in the game you start adding a bit of slack into the final stages of the cast. These are called 'slack line presentations' and there are many fancy casts which fall into this category, though frankly, in real life and in this country, most of them are useless and impractical. You're just not going to risk a curve or a wiggle cast, or a bucket mend, on a large fish whose sight makes your heart pound and hands shake, and that's even before you unhook your fly from the rod ring.

The good news is, there are a lot simpler ways of mitigating drag so that those fancy casts can stay where they belong — on manicured lawns and at fly-casting events — and we can get on with the task of catching or at least engaging with the fish in the most uncomplicated way possible.

Though the drag pulls the fly around in undesirable ways, it actually starts at the rod tip so keeping the rod high after the cast — *high-sticking* — is one of the simplest and most effective methods of minimising drag. Basically, the less line on the water, the less the currents will mess with it.

It follows that if you let the line dangle from your rod tip and allow a belly to form on the water, the current will pull on it and drag the fly, so it is imperative to strip at just the right pace. I call it *stripping at the speed of the current*: as the river brings your upstream cast back at you, you strip the line at the same speed, not faster, certainly not slower.

There is one 'must-have' from the fancy casts repertoire and that's a reach mend where you cast a straight line and at the very end of the cast you lower the rod tip left or right, as dictated by the current, and then, after laying the line on the water, you bring the rod tip back up and fish. This places the line at a more optimal angle to the trout, plus gives you some slack line at the rod tip where it matters most. With just a modicum of practice, reach mend becomes a most natural and accurate cast and you end up using it more often than not.

From my experience, the most important thing about avoiding drag is this: on a sighted fish you only need a short distance of drag-free presentation, in front and over the trout. This is rarely more than one or two metres, and thus relatively easy to achieve, but within this window you need the dry fly to float just right. When you learn to place this window where you want it in relation to the trout your dry-fly fishing goes through an evolutionary quantum leap.

Ultimately, managing drag is about being in touch with your line and fly on the water, seeing what they do and responding accordingly. There are no hard, fast and foolproof formulas because every situation is different. Once you've developed the 'touch' you can present dry flies upstream, downstream, sometimes even across current. This opens up a whole new world of trout

opportunities for you, way beyond anything a formulaic angler can ever get near.

I have seen people 'get' this in a single breakthrough session. One day on my favourite Southland river we came across an epic willow-grub activity which was the first ever for my companion Roeland. We knew the right fly already, so it was all down to the presentation. And with this Roly struggled, dragging the tiny fly, mending too hard, missing the takes. But with a few hints and suggestions, and much of his own focused enquiry, his fishing changed before my eyes, morphing into a whole different style, with much more finesse and precision. The best way I can describe it is that he finally 'connected' to the fly and the line, and soon we lost count of the number of hook-ups.

On the way back, we detoured up a tributary creek and there, rising in the barely perceptible feed line, we saw the best fish of the day. It seemed an impossible proposition: a totally glassy pool, almost no current and a large fish that could spook at a mere shadow of the fly line. Still, soon we were down on our knees, creeping into casting range, and tying on a CDC emerger, a best-guess fly considering how the fish was feeding.

Roly put out a passable reach mend and brought his rod back up to vertical and we watched transfixed as the fly and the fish converged. The trout came up confidently, but in the last moment he refused. The fly must have just started to drag.

'Go again, same thing,' I said and Roly did.

Again, the trout came up to look.

'Drop your rod tip. Now!' I whispered. This bought us another foot of drag-free drift and the trout slurped the fly without hesitation. The perfect take and a lifetime memory. The fish was nearly 5 lbs, though considering the size of the creek it was a sure trophy. Again, as it so often happens during New Zealand dry-fly trout summer, this was fly-fishing as good as it gets.

We still had a long walk back to the truck and somewhere along the way Roly sighed and said: 'Wow, this was a day worth living for.'

And as we walked on, I thought to myself: 'Aren't they all Roly, aren't they all?'

Jennifer too was learning fast, though the progress was anything but linear. She had some casts and presentations so light and accurate — so perfect — that all I could say was 'no one could do it better', and other ones, often on the same fish, that looked like she had tried to throw the fly line out with a broomstick. Funniest thing of all was that she didn't really know how it was happening and why. This, I was to realise, was part of her 'fishing like a girl', best to be left alone and certainly not corrected.

Not that she was not frustrated with it herself.

'Why is it not working?' she would cry out between expletives. 'It was so good on the last fish!'

'Well, you know what to do, you're just not doing it.' I was being as diplomatic as possible. And we left it at that.

It took some doing. Maybe a year later I got an email from her father Brit, a brief fishing report from their outing together on the Crystal River in Colorado.

'You should see Jennifer cast!' Brit concluded his letter.

'I have,' I replied, 'both the good and the bad!'

'There is no "bad" any more,' he wrote back. 'In all the years I've never seen her cast so well. She picked off four fish with just as many casts in tight technical water that even I considered too hard to try.'

I said something like she'd certainly put a lot of work into it. Inwardly, I brimmed with pride, and I would tell Jennifer that because girls love to hear such things.

For now, all that was yet to come and meanwhile, on the West Coast, we had many more of those 'days worth living for', exploring spring creeks, looking for trout. Some days we found a creek literally stacked with fish and we caught too many to mention. Sometimes the fish were so shy as to be almost unapproachable, while other creeks seemed totally devoid of trout. But one enduring and constant theme of our West Coast wandering was the almost unbelievable purity of the waters.

'I don't think I've ever seen trout water this clear,' Jennifer would repeatedly say as we stopped to let our eyes travel up and through another upstream pool. On sunny days, over light-coloured gravels and sands, the trout cast almost theatrical shadows — stark, and black, and sharper than the shapes of the fish themselves — so it felt as if we were looking at trout that had already paired up. But knowing that they weren't, we would often look for the shadows first, which were a lot easier to see, and find the fish from there, then tell how deep the trout was by judging the distance between it and its shadow. On such days, the water seemed clearer than air and you'd swear that except for the rapids and riffles, and the long dreadlocks of weeds swaying in the current, there would be nowhere for the fish to hide.

There is a classic illustrated children's story called *The Snowflake: A Water Cycle Story*, which is a fun and visual way to teach the kids about how water circulates in nature, tracing the journey of a single droplet throughout the year. The snowflake falls down from a storm cloud, melts and disappears underground only to bubble up in a spring. It continues down through farmland and evaporates into the morning fog. It becomes part of a cloud, rains down, gets channelled into a plumbing system where it washes a little girl's face, and flows out to the ocean, to evaporate again and become a snowflake once more.

Jennifer worked as a preschool teacher for a time and so was well familiar with the story. She liked the snowflakes part most — as devout backcountry skiers we both did — and also when the droplet flowed 'into the mouth of great striped fish'. She had frequently taken her schoolkids to the river — out of the story books and into the real world — to teach them about the cycles of bugs and fish, water and trees, and Life in general. And so we agreed that, if you were to illustrate the *Snowflake* story with just one landscape, you could not find a better one than the glacial West Coast.

Okay, so the great fish was not *striped* but *spotted*, but otherwise all the layers were there, from the high-alpine névés to the sea and everything in between was all in front of our eyes in one single image. All we had to do was to turn around to take it all in. Above all, the water in our story was the purest there is — already pure as snow when it fell down on the glaciers and further filtered through forests and moss and the earth itself to become the very spring creeks that we fished.

That night at our camp I asked Jennifer if she knew the adult version of the snowflake story and — surprise, surprise — she had heard of that one too, though not really in any detail. You see, apparently, the snowflakes never quite disappear; they are still there, in a way, even if with a naked eye we cannot see them. But they are only there if the water remains pure and pristine.

It was a Japanese scientist, Masaru Emoto, who came up with the technology to show us this, until now, unknown quality of water. In the controlled lab environment, he would freeze samples of water collected from around the world, and as they began to crystallise into ice, he macro-photographed them via a dark field microscope. The results were astounding.

Though to a naked eye the samples appeared identical, water from pure sources — mountain springs in Japan, the fountain of Lourdes in France, the Mt Cook area of New Zealand, among others — produced perfectly symmetrical and stunningly beautiful snowflake-like crystals, while water from polluted locations, whether rivers or municipal outflows, showed as amorphous blobs, much like close-ups of cancer cells.

Emoto published his findings in the book *The Hidden Messages in Water* which has been translated into over twenty languages and became a *New York Times* bestseller. He went a lot further in his enquiry into the true nature of water, far beyond the scope of this book, and you can follow his work at your own whim, will or curiosity. Suffice to say, he attracted much criticism, ridicule and debunking which is how and why I got interested in his ideas. This may be due to my contrarian nature, but the more someone is debunked the more I'm interested in what they have to say because, living in the world and society that we do, you've got to ask yourself: 'Why would highly educated people, with cushy academic jobs and lifelong careers, spend so much of their time and resources debunking a fool?' Unless there's some inconvenient truth that needs to be covered up, some important knowledge to be kept secret from the masses. In which case, what better way to suppress it than with ridicule?

It comes as no surprise then that Emoto's work struck a lot more resonant chord among the indigenous cultures of the world than it ever did with the mainstream. In Arizona, Hopi Indian

*"Holly sh*t! I can't hold him!" Jennifer getting acquainted with the pulling horsepower of New Zealand trout.*

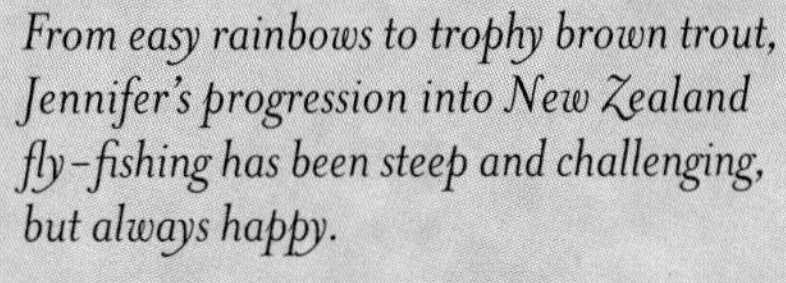

From easy rainbows to trophy brown trout, Jennifer's progression into New Zealand fly-fishing has been steep and challenging, but always happy.

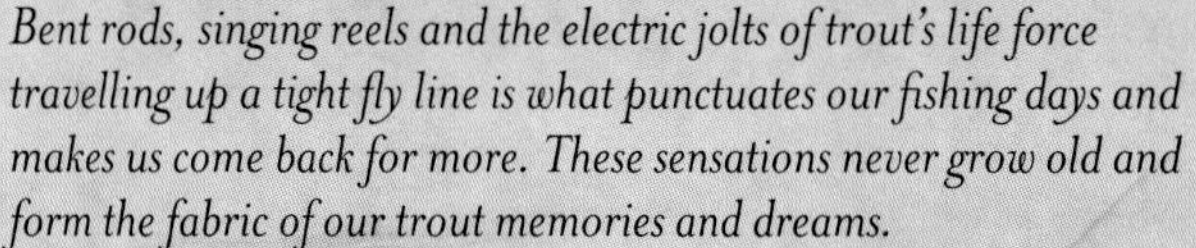

Bent rods, singing reels and the electric jolts of trout's life force travelling up a tight fly line is what punctuates our fishing days and makes us come back for more. These sensations never grow old and form the fabric of our trout memories and dreams.

When a hooked New Zealand trout turns and runs straight at you, stripping or reeling may be too slow and sprinting away from the river is a proven way to keep the line tight. Yours truly, on his way to the nearest Southland town.

Hiking miles of water, looking hard into its structure, and casting only when you see a trout is the essence of fly-fishing in New Zealand. More a trout hunt than fishing, the style is a distillation of the sport, pure and true, as good as it gets and just as hard.

The bursts of rod-bending action and hot-footing after a trout (above) may not be as frequent as elsewhere in the world but every fish here is worth catching, an encounter with beauty and power from which lifetime memories are made.

Efficient, precise and versatile casting is the most critical yet commonly underrated skill in fly-fishing well in New Zealand. Ignore it at your peril!

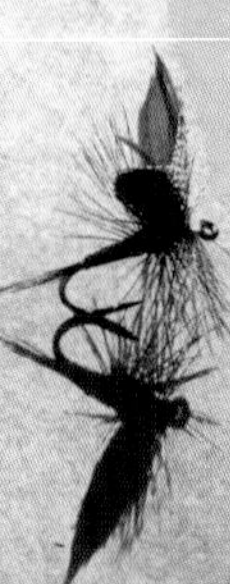

The Fly Fishers International's *casting examiner Mark Huber (top) demonstrates the loose and light rod grip that is necessary for effortless Spey casting. Though relatively new arrivals downunder, double-handed rods and Spey techniques are rapidly gaining popularity in New Zealand, especially on large rivers (middle) and during winter spawning runs of the rainbow trout (bottom).*

Sight fishing from an inflatable standup paddleboard — a SUP — (above) offers not only a fantastic whole-body workout but also an easy access to lake flats and edges impossible on foot. Good SUP fishing skills, like those demonstrated by a fellow convert and top Queenstown guide Chris Dore (bottom left) take time and perseverance to develop but the rewards are plentiful and often large (bottom right).

It is not hard to see that if things keep going the way they are at the moment, in the not too distant future New Zealand may not have trout worth fishing for . . .

elder Vernon Masayesva commented: 'His work helps to show how critical it is to preserve our water resources and to use them properly. What Dr. Emoto has discovered about water is perfectly in keeping with what our elders have told us all along.' Elsewhere, the indigenous reaction to Emoto's research has been a variation on a theme that could be summarised in 'You have proven what our ancestors have been saying. Thank you.'

But beyond its more esoteric aspects, to me the essence of Emoto's work is that he showed us how the degradation of water was not final or irreversible, that the damage of pollution can be undone, the blob returned into a snowflake, something he had also documented in his macro photographs.

Why do I bring all this up in a book about trout? Look at the state of New Zealand rivers today. How do you think they would photograph in Emoto's experiment? As snowflakes or as cancer cells? And which one would you rather choose, because this is largely a matter of collective choice?

I've been writing about water quality and trout since the mid-1990s — and was considered an *alarmist* then — so I won't bore you with repetitions or told-you-sos. Back then, I would rarely hesitate to drink from a river unless it had obviously flowed through a lot of farmland. Now, in many of the same rivers I don't even let my dog go for a swim. Public health warnings about outbreaks of cyanobacteria and *E. coli* now make regular news; worse still are the ones that don't make the news as they can catch you unaware. Even in the backcountry, we now carry a Katadyn filter pump and use it for all our drinking water. It is not hard to see that if things keep going the way they are at the moment, in the not too distant future New Zealand may not have trout worth fishing for — except perhaps in national parks, high above the dairy land — and instead of trout dreams we'll only have memories.

In my three decades on the rivers in this country I have seen degradation of water quality spreading and intensified at an ever-accelerating pace. The decline that used to take a generation or two can now happen in the space of a season and the bureaucrats told us that — in 'clean green' and '100 per cent pure New Zealand' — even *swimmable* rivers are now not realistic. But can you imagine a reality without them? If not, it is certainly high time to start yanking some chains and demanding real-time accountability from the polluters and those who allow it. Rivers are a self-cleaning system; all we need to do is stop messing them up.

And yet, despite being in a crisis situation, it is not all doom and gloom as some commentators would have you believe. Awareness is the only true currency of change and this, in the face of what really amounts to an organised environmental crime, has been growing ever stronger.

For the past twenty years or more all my drinking water has come from a local spring. Sure, at times it's inconvenient and a hassle but, after the initial tasting all those years ago, I would not have it any other way. There is an ornamental trout pool nearby, fed from the same spring, and the trout in it are big, fat and healthy, which for me is alone a good enough indication that the water is still good and safe to drink.

The spring is so popular that most of the time you have to wait your turn to refill your containers. You meet people there, good people, those with awareness of how important quality water is in our lives. One time recently, I was behind a chap old enough to remember the world before modern plumbing. He had a couple of milk crates with him, each with a dozen or so bottles to be filled, and he apologised that he was taking so long. 'But no other way around it,' he said, 'I'm not drinking that crap from the tap. God only knows what's in it. This, young man, is about as good water as you could ever drink.'

You can try to figure the guy's age if a fifty-something seemed young to him, but he was right about the water. It was soft, swirly and cold, and it supported a thicket of vibrant salad-greens below its outlet, much like the West Coast spring creeks. Purest trout water as I've ever seen, though there was no need to state the obvious.

And so I helped the old man to fill the rest of his bottles because others were already lining up behind us.

Even though it was the height of summer, snowflakes, and a lot of them, were about to feature prominently in our lives for the next couple of months. Jennifer's time in New Zealand had run out – how glad she was she didn't just come for a week as originally intended – and she invited me to go back with her to Colorado where deep winter was only just beginning.

Colorado is the size of New Zealand and, with the exception of a band of flatland prairies in the east, most of it is mountains, many reaching or exceeding 4000 metres. The climate is sunny and cold, and winter storms move through quickly dumping huge quantities of exceptionally dry snow. On our first day together on the mountain there was half a metre of fresh powder snow and hardly anyone around. I was in heaven.

The days that followed were a blur of happy exhaustion. It turned out that Jennifer not only fly-fished in the spirit similar to my own, she also had the same 'nose for snow' as I did. Run after downhill run, we streaked through the winter-bound woods of ponderosa pine and aspens, side by side, and keeping each other in peripheral vision but also staying in radio contact as it was easy to get separated, ferreting out the best snow there was on the mountain. I had never known such synergy, and neither had Jen.

'You've brought back my joy of skiing,' she told me one day on the lift. 'After so many years in the mountains I felt I was over it, done it too much. But skiing like this, and with you, makes me realise again just how much I love it.'

'You've done the same for me on the river,' I said.

'Don't you just wish we could fish and ski together for the rest of our lives?'

'Maybe we could.'

Jennifer's face lit up with a smile.

'There's nothing really can touch skiing, is there?' she said. *'The way it feels when you first drop off on a long run . . .'*

'It's too swell to talk about, George said,' I replied.

We were back to the game of trading quotes from our favourite stories and these ones were from Hemingway's short story, *Cross-Country Snow*. Papa Hemingway was perhaps the first, or at least the most prominent, writer to connect fly-fishing and skiing in one lifestyle, showing that, at least when practised in a

Jennifer was right, there was nothing that could really touch skiing, except perhaps a good hatch. But she knew that already.

backcountry setting, both shared similar values and sensitivities and were in fact complementary. After all, if you recall the journey of the snowflake, winter snow is but frozen trout water. The same water we ski in winter we will fish in spring and summer and this gives a well-lived year a beautiful cyclicity.

When I look into the fly-fishing circle of people I know, it is remarkable how many of them are also passionate about backcountry skiing. Some of my guiding friends — Dean Bell would be the first who comes to mind — are so busy during the fishing season the only time I get to be with them is while we ski-tour together in winter. It seems that both skiing fresh snow and fly-fishing share similar set of aesthetics and appreciation of natural beauty. Both encourage an inner enquiry, require high levels of accuracy and precision, if not quite artistry. If anything, skiing not just encourages but enforces these on you: you can goof up a trout cast and laugh about it, but you can't miss a ski turn coming up to a tree or a cliff. The consequences could certainly not be laughable.

At the top of the mountain we got off the lift and headed out of the skifield through one of the backcountry access gates.

'My all-time favourite quote from Hemingway is "Will you have another drink?",' I said to Jennifer.

'I will but let's keep it for après-skiing,' she said. 'I'm thinking pink champagne in the hot tub.'

'You're my dream girl,' I said.

'Awww, you mean it?'

'Like, totally!'

She laughed and pushed off through the gate, found an untracked pitch and dropped down the steep slope trailing a wake of billowing snow, ethereal like cold white smoke. I followed her down, keeping behind and off to one side,

slaloming through the trees, the weightless snow coming up to my waist, sometimes higher. Jennifer was right, there was nothing that could really touch skiing, except perhaps a good hatch. But she knew that already.

For several weeks we lived in this bubble of blissful idyll and when it came to an end, as we knew it would, it was still a shock and a surprise. Denial is more than a river in Egypt and it did not work for us too well in this case. My time in Colorado had run out, I had to go back to New Zealand, to Maya and to commitments that could be neither cancelled nor postponed, and Jennifer's work was also about to claim most of her days. It seemed like we had lived on borrowed time and now came the day to reconcile with reality. And yet we wondered, how come, since we had only really known each other for four months, why did the parting feel so unbearable?

'We need a better plan,' we kept saying to each other, but the parting itself was sad beyond words.

And so, in early February, auspiciously in sync with the start of the cicada season, I found myself back in New Zealand. But even the chirp of the cicadas would not cheer me up; the void caused by Jennifer's absence seemed galactic. Other than work and gathering the strands of my life such as it was before, I needed something else to fully occupy my mind, heart and senses. I needed projects, the bigger, more engrossing and challenging the better.

So how about walking on water?

chapter 4

I LIVE AT THE SOUTHERN LAKES, which are massive bodies of water and full of trout, yet surprisingly they are little fished except by the usual brigade of put-put trollers who tend to stick to predictable lanes and deep water. So the best stretches of sight-fishing shorelines — those with plenty of structure and abundance of food — are rarely touched by anglers. Trouble is, they are also the most inaccessible.

These are the crumbling cliff-lines and natural breakwater shores of giant boulders, overhung with trees and shrubs, hard to get to, even more awkward to follow, not to mention casting from them. The water there is deep-blue or black, with little or no littoral zone and, in season, the trees and shrubs are alive with insects, many of which end up falling into the water. There, just under the surface, large trout cruise in quick zigzagging patterns, reacting to anything that hits the water, examining twigs and leaves, gulping beetles, hoppers or cicadas though never bees or wasps. It is a sight that makes your mouth go dry and sends the heart rate spiking up, for these are not the spooky fish from any popular drive-by river that can shy off at the mere wave of a fly rod, but the top-of-the-food-chain predators worked up to a feeding frenzy, curious and confident. If you've experienced such a sight even once, like me, you'd be coming back again and again, hoping to relive it.

But, as I say, access is a major problem, ranging from hard to dodgy, to impossible. Belly boats and kayaks are next to useless (too low to the surface to see from), motorboats too noisy and clunky. So it all seemed a bit hopeless and limited to a few accessible rocks until, somewhere on the web, I saw a picture of a guy sight-fishing the Florida flats from a stand-up paddleboard. My eyes lit up. Now here was a vessel perfect for the task — stealthy and portable, quick to deploy, ideal to see and to cast from. A few emails later, my fishing-specific inflatable BOTE paddleboard arrived and changed my lake fishing forever.

You have surely seen them around, as stand-up paddleboards — SUPs — have become one of the fastest-growing fitness fads, and for a good reason. As a way of getting into shape, paddling a SUP is right up there with swimming and cross-country skiing, a low-impact full-body workout. You paddle with your arms and upper body, but the power transfer is through your legs and feet into the boat so that all the muscles are engaged. Your legs get stronger, your flabdominals tightened and toned, and as your core strengthens and stabilises — just through mere balancing on the board — a lot of back pains and niggles tend to disappear as well. And it's not like this kind of fitness regimen is a chore, right? You're out there, in fresh air and beautiful places, with a fly rod in your hand. Getting fit while fishing? Definitely my kind of workout.

I'm not saying it's easy, but then most worthwhile things usually aren't. If you just grab your rod and fly vest and hop on a SUP you will most likely spend more time swimming than fishing. Yet with a bit of practice a SUP becomes a remarkably stable fishing platform. The progression is a lot like learning to ride a mountain bike: your balance, turning and propulsion need to become almost second nature before you start fanging down technical trails.

I've put a good few weeks into just paddling, without the rod. This was a revelation in itself because the first thing you notice from the SUP is just how many more fish there are on the flats and shallows than you could ever see from the shore. Cruising the drop-off and looking into the littoral zone it's not uncommon to see several fish at any one time. This flip of perspective — looking in from the outside, from an elevated vantage point and often against a good backdrop of shoreline and trees — is one of the greatest advantages of fishing from a SUP. The others are unobstructed casting space and the stealth of approach. It is the movement that seems to spook the trout most. If you can just drift and keep low and be still, the fish can often swim right under the SUP without scaring off at all.

The easiest way to catch fish from a SUP is to fit it with an accessory tackle rack, secure your rod in there and troll Woolly Buggers and the likes along the flats and drop-offs. The takes are unmistakable, though, at least to begin with, you may want to follow the advice of a fellow SUP-fishing convert, Queenstown guide Chris Dore, and 'always fight the fish on your knees' so that you don't follow them into the drink.

Trolling lures behind the SUP is a good entry-level way to get used to the boat, get a workout and catch dinner, but when you progress to sight-fishing this is another game entirely, one with a lot more moving parts. First, when you put your paddle down to cast, the SUP becomes a lot less stable. A single wake from a passing motorboat or a jet ski can take you out if it catches you unaware. Add to this the excitement of the hunt — the fish moving fast and feeding, you trying to cast accurately to them, often at odd angles, cross-body or backhand — and it's not that impossible to step off the board and truly 'get in amongst them'.

The easiest way to catch fish from a SUP is to fit it with an accessory tackle rack, secure your rod in there and troll Woolly Buggers and the likes along the flats and drop-offs.

Falling in is actually good and part of the learning; just hang on to your rod and clamber back on board. After you fall in a few times you'll be falling off a lot less. Your brain and muscle memory would have figured out the limits of balance and with time and mileage the board becomes like an extension of your body. You'll find you can move around it, even turn, and you won't need to drop down to your knees every time you hook up. In fact, there is nothing quite like the sensation of being towed along by a good-sized fish while with your feet you steer the board so it follows straight. Not exactly wake-boarding but you get the idea.

Good fishing SUPs, like those in the BOTE range, have provision to attach a cooler box. I use a small chilly bin with a couple of bungee cords. This not only keeps your food and drinks cool and handy but, more importantly, makes a good seat to rest on and to fiddle with your fishing gear. It is surprisingly hard to change flies while standing up on the SUP, even in perfectly glassy water — this has to do with how our balance, sight and focus are related — so a simple seat eliminates yet another potential cause of falling in.

At the first few glances, fly-fishing from a SUP may seem too hard and complicated, with a learning progression that involves plenty of blank days. But if you persevere like I did, become comfortable on the board and shake down the procedures — especially the transitions from paddle to rod and back again — in the end it all miraculously comes together and the rewards are beyond measure.

One such day, I put in at a little rocky bay on Lake Wanaka and paddled out to maybe 100 metres offshore. The lake was a glassout as far as you could see, but there was a slight southerly current running and for an hour or so I paddled into it, well away from the shore so as not to disturb the water I was about to fish. Then I turned in again and let myself drift to within casting distance of the shoreline. There was not a cloud in the sky and through the polaroids the water, shaded by the backdrop of the mountains, was inky black. The flashes of gold within it were the big brown trout hunting waterlogged terrestrials.

For the next three hours I drifted along on the barely discernible current, casting to an untold number of trout. This may come as a surprise to many but, per kilometre of the bank, there are a lot more fish in a lake than you'd find in an average New Zealand river. And let me just say I did not get many refusals as most of these trout behaved like they'd never been fished for before. After a while, I even started teasing the fish, pulling the fly lightly along the surface just as they were about to take it. There would be the audible snap of the jaws, a moment of confusion as the trout realised it had missed, then an even more aggressive follow-up take, hard and fast like a punch just under the surface.

It all felt like some kind of surreal fly-fishing nirvana — being surrounded by rising and eager trout, on a perfectly still lake, with no one else around and miles more of shoreline ahead of me. But nothing lasts forever. At one point, looking up to the head of the lake, I saw a nor'west front approaching, a wall of wind, dust and churning water. Within minutes it hit, changing the lake from a glassout to white caps, and the wind-driven swell was smashing metres high against the rocks along which, only moments earlier, the trout fed with such abandon. By then, I was on my knees on the board, surfing my way to the takeout point.

I had learnt my waterman's lessons early during the rookie days on the SUP: the inflatables are a lot more susceptible to wind than solid boards. You need to anticipate the weather and its wind changes and always — always — paddle into them so that you'll get blown back to your takeout, not away from it into the open water, or beyond it, down the rocky shore without a way out for miles.

Back at the truck, deflating and rolling up the SUP into its backpack stuff bag, I had a pang of regret that my fly-fishing nirvana did not last longer. There was so much more water ahead, so many daylight hours, so many more trout to tease. But like the

storm, it was only a passing sensation and did not really matter. If you've been out in the bush and on the water long enough, you know that Nature is always the boss and there is nothing for it but to roll with its whims while making the best calls you can, and besides, as it was, I'd already had one of my best trout days ever.

For the time it lasted, it was like walking on water, with a fly rod at the ready. And should I even mention that I've had many more days like that since?

Later that day I told Jennifer about the trout ecstasy of fly-fishing from a SUP.

'We should try it together sometime,' I said. 'I think you'd really like it.'

'I already do!' she cut in, unable to contain her enthusiasm. 'I have a SUP, solid, not inflatable, and I've been learning to cast from it on our little lake. Never caught a fish yet, but it's a work in progress.'

Somehow, this time, I was not even surprised. We really were on the same page in so many different ways. The big question was: how were we to bring all those pages together into a one cohesive narrative?

chapter 5

WE WERE WALKING UP A WELL-KNOWN RIVER in the Mackenzie Basin, Otto and I, and we weren't seeing any fish. It was the end of February, the tail end of the cicada season when the fishing is easy, and so we already eked out a couple of decent browns by floating big buoyant dries down the current lines and letting the fish find them. A resident of Virginia, and used to fishing small streams and tiny trout, Otto was already elated with the action, like a kid on a dream trip, but quietly to myself I was growing concerned about not seeing any fish.

The day was perfect: sunny and cloudless, and we were walking the high banks and looking down into clear water, along one of the best stretches of the river. And for several hours now we had not seen anything remotely resembling a trout, not even a spooked one. It was unlikely anyone had walked this beat before us, my strategising made sure of that. So why weren't we seeing any fish? I promised Otto sight-fishing, something he had never done before — it seemed on his home waters even during a hatch anglers cast at the water rather than individual trout — and I was not really delivering on that promise. We were fishing, and catching, but *sight unseen*, not quite what I brought him out here for.

Then, suddenly, as we topped the rise of another high bank and looked into the water, there were fish everywhere, the length and width of the entire pool.

'Otto, there's something wrong with my eyes,' I said. 'I'm hallucinating fish! Hundreds of them.'

But he could see them too and so for a long while we stared at the water, mesmerised by the phenomenon neither of us had ever seen before.

Then I remembered. Of course! These were the sockeye salmon on their spawning run. But, for a species not so long ago considered extinct, their numbers were unbelievable. Last season I saw them here in pods of dozens and when I mentioned this to a local farmer he said it was the most of them he'd ever seen in his whole life in the valley. But now, from our elevated vantage point, we were looking at hundreds of fish, and that just in one pool. The bottom shimmered with their green-and-red bodies, the salmon continually jostling and reshuffling, at times scattering in all directions as a newcomer hit the pod, an image reminiscent of a snooker break-off played without skill and too much aggression.

The first time I had seen New Zealand sockeye salmon was during an autumn outing to fish another one of my favourite rivers in the Mackenzie Basin. Just before the trip I happened to read a heart-warming article in *Fish & Game* magazine about how, completely of their own initiative, with a small digger and chainsaws, two local engineers, Ray Newman and Wayne Crisp, cleared and restored one of the historical sockeye spawning streams in the lower Ohau area. I was four-wheel driving en route to my river when I had to ford a stream and, pausing for a moment partway across it, I realised it was *the* stream featured in the article. I stopped and walked a couple of pools and, sure enough, they were full of sockeyes.

But this was late March, and the fish were all black. Their tails and bottom fins were gone, from abrasion against spawning gravels, and the fish, not yet dead but almost, were literally falling apart (like other Pacific salmon, the sockeye all die after their one-and-only spawning run). I vowed to come back earlier another season, to see the fish in their full spawning colours, perhaps try to catch a few of them, but it never happened. Until now.

The problem with trying to catch New Zealand sockeye is that they are not really predators so there is little to no chance of getting them to take a fly. They feed mainly on plankton — swimming in open water and filtering daphnia and copepods with their long and numerous gill rakers — though a 1986 study by the Ministry of Agriculture and Fisheries showed they also eat good amounts of freshwater snails and even bullies. By and large, though, living as they do in the lakes of the Waitaki catchment — Ohau, Benmore, Aviemore and Waitaki — they are not really available to anglers, with only an odd fish being caught here and there, more a curiosity than a targeted quarry. In fact, many people had fished these lakes for years without ever realising there were sockeye salmon living in them.

It is only when the sockeyes begin their spawning run that they become both visible and available to an angler. This lasts only two to three weeks and this is further foreshortened by the fact that, by regulation to protect their spawning, the season for sockeye salmon closes on the last day of February. So, considering that most of the spawning may occur in March, the window of time for catching sockeyes is only a few days' long. Otto and I just happened to be here when it was open at its widest.

Being innocent of human encounters, sockeye salmon do not spook. You can stand above them, tall, visible and casting a fly, and the fish do not consider you a threat. Of course, they don't feed

In a flash he covered over ten metres of fast riffly water to stop just as abruptly face to face with my fly. But he did not take it.

either so the only way to get them to take a fly is to trigger off their aggression by invading their space with a streamer that is both big and gaudy.

I will never forget that first cast to a sockeye for it has given me what no trout ever had. There was a pod of fish below me and among them one actively aggressive male, so bright he seemed almost orange. He was well at the back of the pool, chasing off all incoming intruders. Since you don't aim at individual fish but the entire pods of them, I thought I'd just cast across and down and swing the streamer through to see if there were any takers. The moment my red-and-yellow streamer hit the water the dominant male shot forward to confront it. In a flash he covered over ten metres of fast riffly water to stop just as abruptly face to face with my fly. But he did not take it.

It was a few more casts, this time targeting this one fish and almost tickling his nose with the tail of the streamer before he got annoyed enough to snatch the fly. When he did, I learnt another thing about New Zealand sockeye: they don't really fight. Landing one is like pulling a snag through fast water – steady and hard but without the usual jolts of electricity travelling up the line, from the fish to the angler. If the fight was uneventful, the blurring speed and the raw aggression of his first attack burnt an indelible image in my memory.

Nearby, Otto yelled in surprise as another fish took his fly so hard it nearly pulled the rod out of his unexpecting hands. For a moment we had a double hook-up, one of many.

We fished the long riffle for a couple of hours, merely moving up or down a bit to find fresher fish. Catching them was only a matter of putting out enough casts. These commonly resulted in refusals but often enough a fish more aggressive than most would

These commonly resulted in refusals but often enough a fish more aggressive than most would attack the fly with the violence of a knockout punch.

attack the fly with the violence of a knockout punch. These takes were the most exciting part of it all, and after a few fish, the only exciting part. Landing a sockeye is a mechanical necessity, but since we fished barbless, at times it was enough to let the line go slack for the salmon to unhook itself.

At one point we both reached our fill of catching sockeyes. Chancing upon them, and in such numbers, was as rare as it was unexpected, catching a few was even more so, but catching too many would have diluted the experience. More is not always better. We retired our chewed-up streamers, tied on big dries and resumed our search for trout. Trouble was, we still couldn't find any of those.

Later that day, out of the valley and back in cell reception, I did some impromptu research on New Zealand sockeye because both Otto — who is a vet — and I were fascinated by the river spectacle we had just witnessed and wondering how this enigmatic and only wild southern hemisphere population of *Oncorhynchus nerka* had come back from the brink of apparent extinction so strongly and within only a decade.

It turned out that no one knew more about the local sockeye than their advocate and champion Graeme Hughes, New Zealand's longest-serving Fish & Game officer, who retired in 2018 after forty-nine years of service, and who in his time had seen the sockeye through its heydays, apparent extinction and the remarkable comeback.

Sockeye salmon were introduced into New Zealand in the upper Waitaki catchment in 1901, together with the chinook, under a government initiative to set up a commercial salmon canning industry and inspired by the said industry's boom in British Columbia. The BC anadromous (sea-going) sockeye, reaching

800 millimetres and weighing around 15 lbs, is the staple of the salmon industry, but in New Zealand none of the fish went out to sea (much less came back from there), which prompted Hughes to postulate that perhaps the salmon were not sockeye at all but the kokanee, its landlocked variety. The fact that the introduced 'sockeye' more or less disappeared in the depths of the Waitaki lakes and never grew larger than 3 lbs seems to support his idea.

For nearly seven decades the New Zealand sockeye was considered a complete failure and became nearly forgotten, until 1969 when they were again seen ascending the newly constructed fish pass of the Aviemore spawning race. Larch Stream, in the headwaters of Lake Ohau, was discovered to be their main spawning ground. 'The highest count [was] 18,470 fish in 1979,' Hughes wrote. 'The spawning run and redd excavation occurs in a stream with an average width of five metres and only three kilometres long, an amazing sight.'

But as the Waitaki hydro development surged ahead, the sockeye habitat and population were progressively truncated by more and more dams. This came to a nearly cataclysmic finale in 1982 when the Ruataniwha Spillway was constructed, resulting in dewatering of the entire Ohau River and replacing it with a canal and a series of dams and spillways, cutting the salmon off from Lake Ohau and its headwater spawning creeks. In late summer, thousands of fish gathered at the bottom of the spillway but could go no further. In a major effort to rescue them, some 8000 kokanee were netted and relocated to other Benmore tributaries — Ahuriri, Omarama Stream and the Mary Burn — but this seemed to do no good. 'This relocation failure and the subsequent failure to save the Lake Benmore kokanee appears to have brought about the final demise of this species,' Hughes reported. 'Spawning migrations have decreased drastically, and in some areas kokanee have not successfully spawned for several years. In 1993 spawning season, no kokanee were observed in any known spawning stream.'

Then, in March 2006, the sockeye dramatically reappeared, their return a puzzle and a mystery. Though the reason for this sudden resurgence of a population thought to be almost extinct is unclear, perhaps the local salmon farm — formerly Southern Sockeye Salmon, and now Mount Cook Alpine Salmon — annually releasing 2000 juvenile fish into the watershed since 1993 has played a major part in this turnaround.

In any case, since their reappearance, the numbers of sockeyes seem to be rising almost exponentially, something that, come February and March, trout anglers in the Mackenzie cannot fail to notice. Their massive presence explains a definite absence of trout because, as Graeme Hughes put it, 'when they're moving in the trout are moving out!'.

'Large trout are no match for *Oncorhynchus nerka*, they prefer a quiet existence and tend to keep a low profile while the sockeyes are in the neighbourhood,' he wrote. 'For the angler this makes the trout harder to find and difficult to catch. The sockeye is a pint sized but feisty species [. . .] and should any other fish trespass into its space they are usually driven off, not too far, but the message is clear.'

However, it would be foolish to dismiss the sockeye as a nuisance getting between you and the trout because their true value to anglers goes far beyond being just another fish to add to your species list. They are poor eating once they acquire their spawning colours and they are not really a sporting proposition as a game fish. After you've caught a few as a matter of curiosity you probably wouldn't want to do it again, and to me now, they seem a lot more interesting to look at in the river than to actually catch.

In fact, the sight of hundreds of fish passing and spawning under the Twizel River bridge has become Mackenzie Country's latest tourist attraction.

In fact, the sight of hundreds of fish passing and spawning under the Twizel River bridge has become Mackenzie Country's latest tourist attraction.

You see, great trout fishing and the resurgence of the sockeye are intimately linked, and in the best possible way. In his almost half a century as the Waitaki ranger, Graeme Hughes noted that the watershed of Lake Ohau used to be known for trophy trout, especially 'double-figure' rainbows up to 15 lbs, and that the heyday of that fishery coincided with the highest numbers of sockeye salmon. Once the sockeye numbers went into its near-extinction decline, so did the quality of the Ohau fishery.

'Although the catch of kokanee by recreational anglers is inconsequential the indirect value [of the fish] is the vast food source kokanee fry provide for the trout populations,' Hughes wrote. 'Big fish need big food items and the many thousands of spawning "sockeye" will ensure an ample supply.'

Now, having miraculously come back from the edge of near extinction, the sockeye/kokanee are on the rapid rise again, and not just in Ohau but the entire Waitaki catchment. So watch this space! The Mackenzie Basin already has some of the best trout fishing in the world and there is now every chance that, with tens of thousands, if not millions, of kokanee fry entering the riverine ecosystem, the quality and the size of trout is about to go off the charts.

And we'll all have the resolute pint-size battler to be thankful for it.

chapter 6

'FIRST THINGS FIRST,' Tony Turner told me. 'Come, I introduce you to the dogs, they are the stars here.'

If the dogs wanted to meet me, they did not show it. There were about two dozen of them, all throwing themselves at their short chains, flying through the air in tight arcs, barely touching down before being airborne again. The noise too was like nothing I'd ever heard, between keening of tormented souls and howling multi-part harmonies of a wolf pack readying for a hunt. Yet there was not an ounce of aggression in any of their antics and sounds, just a sheer single-minded drive forward.

'Let's go!' seemed to be both their greeting and an introduction. 'Go, go, Gooooo-uuuu! What's taking you humans so long?'

We were in the carpark of the Snow Farm, New Zealand's only cross-country skifield between Wanaka and Queenstown. Altitude 1515 metres and snow underfoot in every direction you look, the scenery like a piece of the Arctic transplanted onto New Zealand soil, an impression made all the more real by the dogs, all of them Siberian and Alaskan huskies.

As Tony lowered the first sled from the roof rack to the ground, the hellish howls of the dogs went up an octave and doubled in decibels. I held the two lead dogs while Tony hooked up the remaining beasts along the tug-line attached to the sled, which in turned was attached to two snow anchors and the bull-bars of the 4WD for good measure. Tony's tank-like Chevy rocked on its suspension as the dogs yanked at their tethers, crazed with anticipation.

When all dogs were hitched Tony motioned me to get into the sled and when I did he detached us from the truck. Then he pulled out the snow anchors and we shot forward as if from a catapult. At that, the yapping, howling and high-pitched barking instantly stopped and all you could hear was the happy panting of dogs as they shouldered into their harnesses, and the sweet swoosh of sled skis on snow.

We rode along the trail, wide and smooth like a country single-lane, and headed for the wide open horizon, along a creek that was partially frozen and mostly buried under pillows of snow, though here and there you could hear the tinkling and bubbling of unseen water.

We followed the creek until we arrived at the hut in the lee of a large tor, Otago summit rocks that can look like Easter Island sculptures. We staked out, fed and watered the dogs, then got the log fire going and brewed up hot drinks and cooked dinner. We were to stay the night, and the following day we'd hook up again and explore the outlying trails. You could tell that the dogs knew. The tails were already wagging in anticipation.

So what does it all have to do with fly-fishing? Fast-forward six months, to mid-summer when all the snow is gone and the alpine plateau is a sea of golden tussock though the ground is spongy like that of tundra, and I was walking the very same trail with Rick Boyd. We carried fishing rods, 3 wts.

Originally a Canadian, Rick is a fisheries scientist who has spent years in management of the iconic salmon and steelhead rivers in British Columbia — the Skeena, Kispiox and the Dean. He is a keen skier — which is how he first discovered this place — and also a president of the local angling club, and he had invited me to an encounter with an unexpected beauty up here in the tundra.

'Not many people know they are here because you never see them,' he told me, 'they keep mainly in the undercuts so you can't sight them either. But they will come out for a dry fly. Just put your cast along the bank and . . . don't strike too hard!'

Okay, so maybe I was a little too excited, and a good thing too that I'm a fairly accurate caster, because on a strike my first-ever brook trout sailed cleanly out of the water and bounced off the grassy bank behind me before, with another forward cast, I managed to put him back in the creek.

'You got one!' Rick was already running towards me. 'Fantastic! Let's have a look at it.'

The fish was tiny, less than a palm-length long, though for what it lacked in size it made up with exquisite beauty of its markings. It was speckled with carrot-reds and muted golds, and some of the red dots had pale blue halos around them. The leading edges of its bottom fins were edged with pure white, the overall impression was less that of a fish caught and more of a jewel found in a mountain stream.

We caught a few more brookies that memorable first day and after the initial trigger-happy strike I toned down my hook-ups to the size of the fish and the creek. At that time I didn't know that brook trout — more commonly known as brook char or *Salvelinus fontinalis*, and a native to Eastern North America, were introduced in huge numbers into New Zealand beginning from 1877, into every major catchment on the South Island's east coast, and much of the North Island as well. But, mysteriously, they almost all disappeared.

It was thought, and hoped, they may have gone to sea where they would grow bigger, but they did the exact opposite, going upstream into the very headwaters of rivers, into the tussock foothills of the Southern Alps.

'They just don't do well sharing water with bigger and more aggressive trout like rainbows and browns,' Rick said. 'Up here in the alpine, there are no other trout for them to compete with, and only odd anglers like us to ever disturb their peace.'

Even the nature of the land seems to protect the brook trout in this perfect ecological niche. Up here, the tendrils of water which gather from springs, seeps and bogs and which would further down form brooks, creeks and eventually rivers, seem too small and narrow to hold any fish in them but, as Rick showed me, there is more to them than meets the casual gaze.

The tundra ground is soft, sponge-like and easily eroded, and the perpetually running water carves deeply into it. And so the tiny streamlets are more like tunnels, underground pipelines with their tops cut off. What you see from above is only the cut-off opening, maybe less than half-a-metre wide, while below the water is flowing deep, and healthy and plentiful, several times the volume it appears to have from the outside. In those partly open tunnels, the brook trout thrive. I had skied past those creeks numerous times, and never even thought there could be trout in them.

The Pisa Range is not the only place where the brook trout survives. In his PhD work at the University of Otago, Lance Dorsey surveyed and tracked what remains of the 'millions of brook trout [. . .] stocked on both [. . .] islands over a period from 1877–2004', the only such work on brookies ever done in New Zealand.

His conclusions?

They form small and isolated but viable and self-sustaining populations in a few lakes and especially in the high-country headwaters of Otago and Canterbury, well above the waters inhabited by brown and rainbow trout, and they have shown remarkable adaptation to this harsh environment. Dorsey points out that while brook trout can function normally in the temperature range five–twenty degrees Celsius, they are more tolerant of cold than heat stress. Over many generations, their life cycles too adjusted to the alpine environment: they remain small (less than twenty centimetres), mature in their first or second year, and their life span is rarely more than three years.

Lance Dorsey's conclusion was that, in New Zealand, brook trout is 'likely to remain only a curiosity sought by a few dedicated anglers on personal missions [. . . its] appeal more [that of] a piece of living art, its value being purely aesthetic'. This sounded like a perfect project for me, I thought, only that, after an outing with Rick and an email chat with Lance, and while pursuing aesthetics and living art at the same time, I wished for the brookies to put in just a tiny bit more bend in my rod, even if it was the 3 wt. For this, and it's no secret, there is only one place in New Zealand, a high-country lake in Hakatere Conservation Park, inland from Ashburton.

Fast-forward another year and I was approaching this very lake with my fishing compadre Craig Sommerville. Craig grew up on Scotland's best salmon rivers and he has a passion for streamers and Spey rods. We just spent three days prospecting for salmon on the fly in both the Rakaia and the Rangitata rivers, but since the salmon weren't there I'd figured we could boost the morale with a few nice and easy fish like the brookies. After all, as one last-century angler commented, they were 'too easily caught by anything with red and did not offer much of a fight'. Just the kind of fish we needed after three blank days.

Craig is one of the best anglers I know, though he's so modest you'd never guess it until you see him in action. The same goes for his cooking.

'Can you cook?' I asked him before our first ever multi-day outing. 'I only go on road trips with people who can cook at least as well as I do.'

He rolled his eyes but said nothing. I was yet to find out that he was a Michelin-star chef as well.

The day could not have been better — sunny and still, without even a hint of clouds. The lake was set into the golden tussocks and encircled by mountains and, around it, the stillwater bugs were buzzing with summer fervour and intent. There were extensive shallows with tussock-head islands which made for mushy flats, sections of deeper water over gravels and rock structure, but the main feature of the lake was a forest of underwater weeds towards the centre.

We took a side each and started to fish. Visibility was perfect, insect life prolific. Since there was nothing rising, we fished small streamers, casting them out far, then stripping them bully-style — short, sharp and with plenty of pauses, allowing for the stillness of the lake — all the while keeping our eyes on the surface. Maya's eyes

But it was the same perfection, minus the fish, or to paraphrase the title of John Gierach's memorable book, it was 'Still Life without *Brook Trout'.*

were glued to it too; she was coiled with anticipation to spot and point any rises for us.

But for hours nothing happened, not on the surface, not beneath it. By then, Maya had built herself a nest among the clumps of tussock and was busy napping, and in the afternoon heat this seemed like a lot more productive use of time than thrashing lifeless water.

We were coming back to the camper, hot, tired and more than a little dispirited, when we were intercepted by a local man on a day-long mountain-bike ride.

He enquired how we got on.

'There's no fish in here,' I said.

'Oh yes, there are!' the man's face was all smiles and good cheer. 'I got a nice four-and-a-half-pound brookie here last week, and I know of bigger ones caught recently. You just got to keep at it. A little bit of wind helps, too.'

He waved and cycled off on his cross-country mission and we powwowed what to do next.

'Since we're here, may as well give it another go tomorrow,' Craig said. 'Could be a totally different day.'

We stayed and camped near the lake. Single malt with a good friend under the dome of starlight is a cure-all to any angler's woes and so the next morning we sieged the lake with renewed enthusiasm. But it was the same perfection, minus the fish, or to paraphrase the title of John Gierach's memorable book, it was 'Still Life *without* Brook Trout'.

Totally dejected, we packed up and changed watersheds and, in short order, found both large brown trout feeding on big dries, and even bigger chinook salmon, holding resolute in the flow of glacial water. The latter would not take our flies — the pods would open up, individual fish swing sideways to let our flies pass — though all of this is a part of another narrative. The brookies eluded us completely and it was not before a couple of seasons passed that I mustered enough enthusiasm to revisit the lake.

When I did, it was a cold blustery day, the kind you are warned about in the backcountry. This was by choice because it appeared by all accounts and reports the lake fished best when the weather was bad. I reasoned that, during our previous visit with Craig, the water must have been too calm, and perhaps too warm, and since we never saw a fish or even a sign of one, it was fair to conclude the brookies sought refuge in the depths of that weed forest at the centre of the lake, and this would have made them both invisible and completely out of our reach.

This time, the nor'wester ripped down the lake, pushing waves and wind lanes, and churning up the water. I figured the windward shore would be where the food would accumulate and so I positioned myself there and side on to it, letting the wind and the waves swing my streamer in a downwind arc.

It is satisfying to come up with a fly-fishing theory that actually works, when the results prove your logic, especially if you have been humbled on previous attempts. After only a few casts, I felt a solid tug on the line and I had my first good-size brookie, then another, and another.

They were all in the three-pound range, their skin strongly marbled, the colours muted but for those unmistakable white fin edges. All three were in superb condition, clearly making a good healthy living in this harsh and remote place.

Brook trout *are* easy to catch, and they don't put up much of a fight, merely shaking their heads and lacking both strength and stamina to take out much of the line. They won't earn you bragging rights and they don't make good subjects for hero photos unless you're incredibly short. But they live in beautiful places, and they seem to mirror that beauty back, magnified and distilled.

When Jennifer told me that, of all the diverse fish she's chased — from cutthroat trout to tarpon — the brookies are some of her most favourite, I knew we were on the same wavelength, for the little fish somehow embody what we seek. Art, curiosity, wonder, personal missions, and long hikes in remote places.

For me, the very essence of fly-fishing.

chapter 7

MY BIGGEST PROJECT BY FAR BEGAN WITH A FEAST. Under a peach tree, in the garden of a Lake Hawea home, a table was set, the silver cutlery glinting with purpose. I'd shredded an Italian salad mix onto the plates, propped it with sun-dried tomatoes, black and green olives, cubes of salty goat-milk feta and Whitestone Brie, and imbued the lot with avocado oil and dried wild thyme. As a follower of Slow Food movement – the global counter-current to the deluge of fast food and all it represents – I take time and care preparing meals, always hoping for a little alchemy to occur, a little sensory magic, such that the taste transcends the sum of the ingredients.

I'd been elaborate with the sauce, too, marinating three handfuls of prunes and figs overnight in brandy, then simmering them in red wine with a cinnamon stick and raw honey, and thickening the result with stone-ground flour. I'd allowed a bottle of shiraz to breath the late-summer Otago air, well away from the coal-fired barbecue, which also was quietly warming up for business. When all was ready, my visitor produced a bowl brimming with cubed venison, and he tossed its contents on to the gridiron amid much sizzle and smoke. The fire worked its transformation. Moments later we ate.

Sure, I'd had venison before, but I'd only ever considered its taste, not wondering about its source or the effort that went into obtaining it. This time it was going to be different, which is how a seemingly ordinary dinner turned into a life-changing communion.

This venison came with its own story, and we heard it while we ate. It was of a man hiking up a mountain valley for several hours, then spending a cold, uncomfortable night among the ferns on the edge of a forest clearing. The man didn't dare to light his gas cooker during the coldest predawn hours lest the fumes announced his presence. Instead, he rose stiffly but silently, slipped a live cartridge into his rifle, then crept stealthily along the bush edge. The deer – a spiker – didn't sense him coming, and the man, with his sniper's eye, watched the animal feed for a long while before pulling the trigger, shooting the deer dead, cleanly, just behind the shoulder. The killing marked a turning point in the story, the end of its first and easy act.

Act two had the man slinging a pulley in a tree, hoisting the carcass off the ground and removing all the meat he thought he could carry out. Since he believed the 'carcass should rattle when the hunter has finished with it', he had more than he could manage, but, detesting waste, he was determined to try anyway. Thus, although its recounting understated the fact, Act three was the longest. It featured the man returning home, the contents of his backpack — nearly as heavy as himself — reluctant, it seemed, to leave the valley. There was a swift river to be crossed several times using a manuka pole for stability, sidles above crumbling bluffs, and the plain step-by-step drudgery of negotiating a narrow overgrown trail. The entire journey felt like a long and excruciating penance for taking a life.

Yet the man had not taken life thoughtlessly or for so-called recreation. He knew the deal, thus he toiled stoically. He knew his story would have many good endings, as many as the number of dinners that could be gleaned from a fully grown deer, which was a lot. During frequent rests, he thought of the generations of New Zealand hunters before him, particularly the professionals who'd shot deer to sell the meat and who'd been required by veterinary and hygiene regulations to carry out the beasts whole, hooves, guts, antlers and all.

That, he thought, made *The Old Man and the Sea* look like a doddle. A full day shouldering a deer of 100-plus kilos through trackless bush and across gullies, scree slopes and rivers would quickly sieve out the wannabes. Face to face and skin to skin with his prey, the sweat of the one mixing with the blood of the other, a hunter truly got to know the hunted. He earned every cent he eventually got for his deer.

Such thoughts eased the man's burden. They filled in the time, shortened the distance. Still, it took him nearly six hours to get back to his car, another half day to divide the meat into appropriately sized portions, each in its own labelled freezer bag. Now, dining merrily under the peach tree, we were living out one of the story's many satisfying endings, but this, oddly enough, only left me feeling more hungry than before. The generically encoded urge of the hunter began to awaken within me.

In my efforts to live a rounded sample of human experience I'd somehow missed that part, the hunter–provider going bush to feed his family. So far my provider's instinct had manifested itself in the hunt for trophy magazine assignments and fly-fishing gigs, the butchering of the resultant cheques, and returning home loaded with groceries and other consumables. Now I saw there was a way to shorten the food chain, to bypass the middleman, the barcodes and the price tags. With the taste of venison still fresh in my

Then, a sworn pacifist and decrier of arms, I found myself cat-footing through the forest, peering through the cross hairs of a scope.

memory, in short succession I acquired a firearms licence, a rifle and a stack of how-to books. Then, a sworn pacifist and decrier of arms, I found myself cat-footing through the forest, peering through the cross hairs of a scope.

I was already a hunter — albeit, a trout hunter. Yet so many times in the past, while hiking rivers to fish them, I literally walked into red deer — waking them up from where they had bedded down for the day, seeing them crossing rivers not twenty metres in front of me and pausing mid-current to look back at me, finding them bluffed on rocky benches across the creek I was fishing and taking so long to get off I could have taken them all down several times over. So, with all that in mind, how hard could it be to bring home a deer, right?

The more I looked into it, the more I was also fascinated with the story of deer in New Zealand, one of uncommon interest and complexity, and unrivalled elsewhere in the world. To begin with, it came as a complete surprise that the adventures of my visitor and culinary compadre had taken place among the hills I saw every day above the shrubs that enclosed our garden. Not only were there wild deer all around us, but Lake Hawea was one of the locations where deer were introduced into the country, seeding what later become known as the Otago herd.

Like the release of trout and salmon, the introduction of deer was a concerted effort to anglicise a foreign land, to make it more like home by populating it with useful and familiar beasts. But though driven by the well-to-do gentlemen of leisure who presided over the numerous acclimatisation societies, the liberation of deer brought about a liberation of another sort — a minor class revolution.

Written into the societies' charters was an illustrious provision that, unlike in the motherland, where deer-hunting was the preserve of aristocrats and poachers, in the new land 'hunting and fishing [were] to be easily available to everyone regardless of wealth or status'. Nonetheless, at first, hunting and fishing were not allowed on Sundays, the only day the working class had to engage in leisure activities.

Animals were readily available from the game parks and estates where the English and Scottish nobility had kept and bred semi-wild deer for generations — exclusively for trophy heads on stags. Make what you will of head-hunting, this was the motivation for bringing deer to New Zealand. The first arrival was a red-deer stag from the Royal Park in Richmond, which was released in Nelson in April 1854. Three more red deer from Thorndon Hall arrived in 1861, and these were supplemented with animals from Warnham and Windsor parks.

The animals were crated and fed on clover, hay and carrots during the two-month ocean journey. A number died en route, but those that survived proved to be of sturdy stock indeed. Once the transportation procedures had been perfected, red deer were liberated in all the main forested areas between Auckland and Stewart Island, often with rapid success. For example, the first Lake Hawea release, in 1871 — two stags and six hinds of wild Highland stock — went so well that in 1913 Warnham Park imported six hinds from the region to beef up its own stock.

Red deer (*Cervus elaphus*) spread rapidly, finding the country much to its liking. It colonised every available patch of habitat, particularly the inaccessible mountain valleys, where it remained undisturbed for decades. A number of other deer species — there are some sixty worldwide — were also brought to New Zealand but none matched the tenacity and phenomenal adaptability of the red deer. With the abundance of winter feed in the evergreen forests, *C. elaphus* hinds could become pregnant as yearlings, at least a year earlier than in their native land. Within only a few decades of the species' introduction, New Zealand stags began sporting much longer and more impressive antlers than their UK forefathers, and by the 1930s New Zealand had become firmly established as the top deer-hunting destination in the world.

Yet, at the same time, it was becoming evident that the deer were doing too well too quickly. The selective trophy hunters — still largely the visiting British upper class — noticed that the quality of the antlers was steadily deteriorating, while the local meat shooters reported seeing large herds of thin, emaciated deer. You may recall from my *Trout Diaries*, a similar thing happened to Taupo trout, when the population crashed after the first golden era of trophies. But when it came to red deer, a lot more disturbing was the widespread damage to the forests. In large tracts of native bush the entire understorey had gone, the forest floor stripped bare, while the canopy was a drying carapace, a vestige of its former splendid self.

New Zealand's forest trees evolved in the absence of large-hoofed animals, and their roots are often close to the surface. Once the protective cover of mosses, ferns and humus was disturbed, the roots were exposed and prone to damage from trampling, while every branch or shoot within reach offered good browsing. Under this assault the forest cover thinned and the land began to erode. Rainfall gouged the steep mountainsides, deepening the gullies until they collapsed, washing the soil from the land, exposing the underlying rock-beds and scree slopes, clogging up trout rivers with silt. The deer were leaving a nascent moonscape in their wake. And they were constantly on the move, searching for pastures new. Wildfires could not have wreaked more persistent damage.

In Canterbury and Otago, starving deer were coming out of the bush, encroaching on farmland, competing with stock for grazing. Mobs of hundreds were reported, the largest of 400 animals. A few years later the situation had become a crisis and the noble beast had plummeted from grace. It was declared a pest, a menace and a plague. A price was put on its head, but the bounty scheme had a negligible effect on the overall population. The gamekeepers realised that the situation was completely out of control, and by 1930 they had lifted all protection from red deer, initiating wholesale culling, which quickly took the shape of a military operation.

In the ensuing fifty-year Deer War, some two million animals were shot and fortunes and legends made. An entire subculture was born, one that left the country with the legacy of an untold number of backcountry huts, a scattering of seemingly impossible landing strips in the most remote valleys, and the iconic figure of the can-do Kiwi deer hunter. The last of these was a larger-than-life foot soldier in shorts, Swanny and perpetually wet boots, who was posted to live in the bush for months at a time to save the country from pestilence, and who openly admitted there was nothing else he'd rather do. It was the red deer, and the trouble it caused, that brought out the 'good keen man' in many a New Zealander and ushered in what its participants called the Last Great Adventure. Among Kiwi men, the nostalgic longing for those days has never really faded.

'After a job, eh son?'

'Yes sir.'

'Done any hunting before?'

'Too right! Been after goats and pigs in the Hunuas for years!'

After an examining pause. . .

'We pay you seven-pounds-ten a week and ten bob a skin. We supply all the ammunition, but if you use more than three rounds a kill, you pay for them. Anything else you want to know. . .?'

No sir, other than . . . where do I sign. . .?

Thus did legendary bushman Barry Crump, underage and under-qualified, lie his way into his dream job. So, too, began *A Good Keen Man*, his decidedly low-brow account of a deer culler's life, a tale that both encapsulated and preserved the quintessential, and often secret, dream of New Zealand men — to go bush with a .303 Long Tom and a dog, to cook on a campfire and eat out of a sooty billy, to drink gumboot tea that smells of wood smoke, and to answer to no one but the call of the wild.

The exploits of the deer cullers, their tallies, lifestyle and adventures, have long since become the staple of Kiwi bush lore, but often the legends were shy in the making. Author Jack Lasenby once recounted in a videotaped interview how, being a complete hunting greenhorn on the prowl on the open slopes above Lake Waikareiti, in today's Te Urewera National Park, he wasn't entirely sure about the identity of his first target. He scoped the animal for fifteen minutes, unable to decide if it was a deer or a Jersey heifer. After he'd finally fired a shot, he ran up to the downed animal, his heart in his mouth.

'Christ,' he said, 'I hope I haven't shot a cow.'

There were many government cullers before and after Crumpy who, like him, lied their way into the job, overstating their age, bush experience and hunting abilities. As they recall it today, those were the innocent days, when you could make it up as you went along, when you didn't need a building consent to put up a tent, when it was more the bush lawyer than the red tape that barred your way. The cullers valued a no-nonsense practicality and self-reliance, and those who stayed on became exceptionally skilled, hunting down thousands of deer, holding the fort against the environmental disaster the animals spelt.

The job was undeniably attractive: you were in the hills, free and your own boss, and paid to hunt. The money was good, too. In the 1940s, when the average weekly wage was around £6 ($12), Rex Forrester, a lifelong hunter, one of the original fishing guides in New Zealand, and the prime chronicler of the era, recalled selling fifty deer skins — the result of one bush trip — and grossing himself and his partner £50 each. The culling season ran from the beginning of November to the end of May, and the men left the bush only to bring out skins and to replenish their supplies. The top guns regularly shot more than a thousand deer in a season.

As always, hunting and shooting were the easiest parts of the job. The skins, and later — when a market for wild venison was discovered in Germany — the meat, had to be carried out to the road, in the early days on a man's back or a pack horse, later with the aid of any capable contraption. Trolleys, buggies and jetboats were all used to ease and speed up the transport of deer carcasses; tractors were disassembled, flown up into remote valleys like the Upper Wilkin and Siberia, and put together again. Aircraft were used initially to parachute supplies, but hunters soon realised that, with a degree of skill and even more daring, they could be used to carry out the deer as well. Several men promptly obtained pilots' licences and bought their own aeroplanes.

One of these was Alan Duncan, a member of the original Crumpy's bunch in the Urewera and considered — if such distinction can be awarded — the best hunter New Zealand has produced. He bought a Piper Super Cub, then went round the aero club to find someone who could show him how to fly it. Before long, Dunc — as he was known — flew the Cub to his Makarora home, on the edge of Mount Aspiring National Park, and began to put the machine through its paces, finding its absolute limits, then backing off just a little. Over the years he constructed some twenty-one airstrips, many of which would give today's Civil Aviation Authority officials a cold sweat and palpitations.

'They were one-way strips,' he commented matter-of-factly.

'Once you committed you had to land, or you pranged the plane.'

Though there seemed to be no end to the hunters' ingenuity, courage and perseverance, there was also no end to the deer. Even with such valiant efforts (the record tally for one man on foot in one day was 101 deer) the campaign was seen as a failure, for the ecological crisis caused by deer overpopulation showed little sign of easing. It was becoming evident that foot soldiers alone could not win the war.

The solution — helicopter hunting — was already on the horizon, but it wouldn't be fully implemented until the mid-1960s, when the *Christchurch Press* carried a telling advertisement: 'Deer-stalkers — We want your deer and pay 13d per lb gross weight on all carcasses. . .' Before long, deer hunting would become a veritable gold rush.

A Good Keen Man spoke from one heart to another, and therein lies the book's unfading popularity. The adventurous hunting spirit that haunts its pages, though no longer spurred by financial gain, is still alive and well. It has withdrawn from the limelight, however, since today's sophisticated society, while still craving meat, prefers it in neatly packaged morsels from the supermarket or deli, and despises hunting as a barbarian blood sport. Still, it bears noting that there are some 468,000 firearms holders in New Zealand, most of whom do not frequent shooting ranges. They own their shotguns and rifles for more practical reasons, such as hunting deer and living the life of Crumpy, if only for the odd weekend.

The hunters' hut on the bush-line of the southern slopes of the Garvie Mountains, between Southland and Otago, could well have been a relic from the cullers' days were it not for its uncommonly tidy appearance, courtesy of my host and guide, Gary. When we arrived there one crisp late-season evening astride a farm quad bike, the hut and the creek it stood beside were thickly hoar-frosted, but before long a large open fire was roaring under a desk-size grate and the flames were licking a blackened billy suspended from one of numerous S-shaped hooks.

I'd met Gary one spring during a regular early-season fly-fishing forays. He was working full-time as a fencer on a large Southland station, and fished all other hours remaining in his week so we'd fallen into easy conversation. This led to dinner at Gary's that night, and he'd served venison back steaks, the best the land had

. . . he had honed his skills to such a degree he'd turned to hunting with a bow, since, as he told me, shooting a deer with a rifle was no longer enough of a challenge.

to offer. Timidly I'd asked him if he'd show me how to hunt. Gary was a quintessential Kiwi bushman – sharp, experienced and competent, and making no fuss about any of it. Hunting the shy whitetail deer around Stewart Island, he had honed his skills to such a degree he'd turned to hunting with a bow, since, as he told me, shooting a deer with a rifle was no longer enough of a challenge.

It would prove plenty of a challenge for me, however. I already sported a Wetherby eyebrow, a greenhorn's giveaway that you acquire when the eyepiece of your scope leaves a distinct purple mark on your forehead as a result of recoil. Still, Gary assured me there were lots of deer around. It shouldn't be too difficult to bring one home.

The Garvie Mountains, dotted with megalithic rocky outcrops known as tors, and with golden tussocks softening their gentle curves, are the classic Otago hills. Patches of beech forest that cling to the folds and creases of the land provide ideal habitat for red deer. The tops are less a range of rocky summits than a series of rolling plateaus covered with tundra-like vegetation and spongy peat bog. At that time of year this surface layer was frozen solid and crunched underfoot like a carpet of Weet-Bix. Deer sign was plentiful: chewed-off stubs of celmisia leaves, hazelnut-like droppings, countless hoof prints.

Gary had thrown a surprise bonus to this outing: not far from the hut there was a backcountry creek which, because of complicated access, was rarely fished. High above it and paralleling the creek was a disused water race from the days of gold mining and we could walk the race — smooth like a hand-built mountain-biking trail — and spot the trout from up high, and when we saw one, we'd come down and try to catch it. A combination of polaroid glasses and binoculars worked remarkably well, and besides — unmolested by anglers — the trout were out in the open and easy to see from above.

And so we fished the days and hunted the twilight hours, when the deer are most active, a mix as perfect as it was complementary. Why didn't I put the two together before?

At dawn, with Gary's black curly-coated retriever, Prue, roaming around us, we walked slowly along the bush margins, frequently pausing to glass the hillsides ahead. Red deer were fringe dwellers, Gary explained, only coming out into the open when they felt secure, usually at first light and then again at dusk. On the open hilltops around us, they often sought out high vantage points from which to survey their territories and watch for any approaching danger. Indeed, I soon spied an enormous set of antlers silhouetted against the skyline. Its owner was regarding his kingdom with an alert gaze. Below, a herd of hinds grazed contentedly.

'I've never managed to get close enough to that guy,' Gary said, his words both tinged with regret and carrying the hint of a promise.

A deer's eyesight was on a par with ours, though more sensitive to movement than colour, Gary went on as we sneaked from one rock to the next, the soft downhill breeze always in our faces. Its nose and ears, however, were as good as a dog's. There were plenty of deer in sight, but despite our utmost care and stealth we couldn't quite get within shooting range, which in that country was something less than 300 metres. We would see a herd of deer, agree on an approach route and a rock from which to shoot, then creep on our way, out of the animals' sight and with a favourable wind. Yet each time we reached our prospective ambush position the deer had already moved on and were again just beyond firing range. It was as if they sensed us in some uncanny extrasensory way.

We fished the rest of the day, when the sun was high and the light good, and returned to the forest edge at dusk for another session.

It was then that Gary spotted a pair of ears in the sea of tussock. Just that — two ears more than 300 metres away — yet an unmistakable sign that at least one deer was resting there. We crawled to the nearest rock, and I lay down to take aim. Gary whistled and the deer stood up abruptly to investigate the noise. The cross hairs of my scope followed the inside outline of its foreleg and rested on the area of lungs and heart. I pulled the trigger.

An almighty BANG reverberated among the weathered rock, then faded, and the deer still stood there, looking in our direction with surprise. When it finally realised what had happened, it broke into a trot, and out of the tussock several other animals burst into view and followed it. It all took place in an instant, and Prue shot forward like a second round, ready to lock on to the scent should an animal have been wounded.

She returned twenty minutes later, tongue lolling, a puzzled, almost questioning, expression in her faithful eyes. No scent. No deer. I had missed, at about only 130 metres. I vowed revenge against my own ineptitude. I have so often given people hell about their fly-casting but look who was talking! I would go home and practise until I could shoot the pupils out of countless bullseye targets, blow the flames off candles, or whatever it was that hunters did to improve their marksmanship. I swore to return during the silly season, when during spring yearling spikers are forced out of the herds — Nature's way of dispersing the population — and they straggle and blunder around, unsure what to do with themselves, curious, goofy and inexperienced, and thus make easy prey. At least I'd be faced with equally asinine quarry. The odds would be more even.

Gary was neither fazed nor disappointed. 'It won't have been the last time you'll miss.' It was just the rookie's rite of passage. The way fishing wasn't just about catching a fish, he said, there was more to hunting than shooting an animal. A lot more.

In gathering cold and darkness, we returned to the hut, taking a short cut through the forest, making use of the extensive network of deer trails.

Overnight, as it is not uncommon for inland Otago, it snowed to low levels — genuine brass-monkey weather. No self-respecting deer would be out in such conditions, Gary concluded, and called a retreat. We drove back into a stinging southerly blizzard, getting the quad stuck up to its belly, dragging it free, slip-sliding down steep greasy hillsides, at every opportunity slapping our hands to stave off the cold-induced numbness. Later that day, sitting in the warmth of Gary's home, with hypothermia safely at bay but teeth still chattering, I began to understand why at my local shop venison was going for nearly

$40 a kilo. Considering the effort involved in getting it there, the price seemed fair and reasonable.

Back in the 1960s, it was the rising price of venison and the discovery of new markets for it, combined with new ways of hunting, that in the end won the war against deer and stopped the destruction the animals were causing. Suddenly, the deer was no longer a pest but a valuable natural resource to be harvested. Across the country, deer hunting gathered so much momentum that within a few years it became a multimillion-dollar industry.

In 1963, Tim Wallis — best known today as the creator of the Warbirds Over Wanaka air pageant — and fellow entrepreneurs began experimenting with helicopters to recover deer in the Matukituki Valley, near Mount Aspiring. The hunters were still on foot, shooting deer and bringing them into the open, but they no longer had to carry the animals out. A helicopter could do that, first with side racks, then, when this proved clumsy and inefficient, with cargo nets and strops.

Within minutes tons of fresh venison could be down on the valley floor where the freezer trucks were waiting. Wallis immediately knew he was on to a good thing; the rest was just details. He mortgaged himself up, bought a helicopter and promptly crashed it, writing the machine off. Undeterred, he asked the bank for another loan and soon had his second chopper. Time was precious because around the country other hunters were quick to catch on, and soon there were helicopter operations wherever there were deer in sufficient numbers. What followed was all-out war against *C. elaphus*, a culling unprecedented in the history of the world and unlikely ever to be repeated.

It wasn't long before the hunters realised it was much more economical to shoot directly from the helicopters than from on the ground; choppers thus became gunships, armed with semi-automatic weapons. Deer could now be hunted in previously inaccessible areas. They could be flushed out of the bush and mustered, then mowed down by the shooters, while empty shells pinged off the whirring rotors.

The tallies of the era were phenomenal. By 1968, hunter Mike Bennett had shot 10,000 deer, while Jim Kane shot some 40,000 in four years. When, in 1967, Wallis went to hunt in

Fiordland, he had his own aircraft carrier — the steamer *Ranginui*. Her masts and derricks had been removed to accommodate two helipads, and her interior had been converted into a giant freezer. Wallis's team averaged ten deer an hour. It took only three days of hunting to fill the ship.

Equally remarkable were the feats of the pilots. Working out of Taupo, pilot Joe Keeley had his helicopter booked for the routine fifty-hour check every Monday morning, while *Ranginui* pilot Bill Black had to have his checked every three-and-a-half days. The machines were pushed to their limits and beyond. Red-lining — revving the engine into the red — while lifting off with a heavy load was a common practice. Smaller helicopters, such as the Hughes 300, had to be on the edge of a cliff to get airborne when fully loaded. The pilot used the torque of the engine to lift off, spiralling up, then dropping, the rotors often bending upwards. It was a controlled fall, a one-way trip, at the end of which the cargo net had to be released the instant it touched the ground or it could pull the machine to earth with it.

The boom peaked in 1973, when some 140,000 deer were shot and airlifted out. Just about anything that could fly was in the air, hunting, and some 100 helicopters were competing with each other. Even in the most remote areas no deer was safe.

Inevitably, the deer rush took a heavy toll on both men and machines. Between 1976 and 1982, 208 helicopters crashed while hunting. Seventy-two of those machines were totalled. Wallis's operation lost nine helicopters in one year, and hunter Charlie Jelly commented that 'if you walked away from a crash it was a good landing'.

Soon enough New Zealand no longer had a deer problem, but the hunters did: market demand for venison was still high and they were running out of animals to shoot. All the easy deer were long gone and the survivors had grown cunning. Pursuit of a few deer was uneconomic given the prohibitive costs of running a helicopter. This, in turn, led to live capture of deer and the establishing of deer farming, from which most of us get our venison today.

The New Zealand deer story has many more chapters and turns, like the development of the net gun for live capture of the animals from helicopters (which has since been used around the world for capture and relocation of moose, bison, caribou, elk, wolf and their likes), and the creation of game hunting estates where, under totally controlled 'behind the wires' conditions, foreign gentlemen of means can shoot themselves trophy stags — chosen from a catalogue of many — at their leisure, say, between lunch and afternoon cocktails. Yes, I know what you're thinking. Me too. Just think how mad we would all get if this happened to our trout fishing!

You can follow these stories at your own whim and pleasure, and meantime, I'm still hunting for my free-range venison. I am at the stage of a 'guided hunter' — though never *behind the wires* — and so whenever I go with someone experienced we find deer and sometimes bring one or two home. But when I go out on my own, there seems to be not a deer to be found in the whole God's own New Zealand. This, I'm told, is a passing phase, much like a newbie angler yet unable to see the trout even if they are plentiful.

Overall, I've found deer hunting a lot harder than fly-fishing for trout. More senses and finesse are involved, a lot more stealth. A trout may see you at ten to fifteen metres and spook, but a deer can smell you from half a kilometre away and just ghost into the forest and you'll never know it was even there.

But it's good to be a rookie again, and there is so much to learn in this game. I know when I finally go into the bush all on my own and come out with a deer it'll be like a graduation in an ancient art, a genetic realignment with who we still are. Plus, pride and achievements aside, it's going to taste really, really good.

chapter 8

AT DUSK, ON THE UPPER WAIAU RIVER, the mayflies were hatching. They swarmed off the water like some surreal upward rain, each insect a droplet dimpling the surface first, rising as if in slow motion along a hyperbolic flight path, vanishing into the glowing Southland sky.

The river was at its extreme high, flowing hard and fast right up against the rainforest. All gravel beaches were gone and the only way to try to fish was to clamber atop one of the bankside boulders — slippery with wet moss as if glazed by ice — and cast sideways, using the downstream for a backcast and placing an oversized artificial anywhere into the explosive spectacle of the hatch.

Almost all of their lives — usually a year, sometimes two in case of the larger species — the mayflies spend underwater among the rocks of a streambed. Then one day, when everything is just right, they ascend to the surface to hatch. There, they struggle through the viscous membrane of the water and climb out of their nymphal shucks — think of a kayaker, adrift in a current, pulling herself out of a tight cockpit. Then they fly off, unusually for insects keeping their bodies vertical in flight, tails trailing like long legs, giving an overall impression of dainty ballerinas carried on gossamer wings. Once in the air, they live only a day or two, to mate, procreate, and to die and to fall back into the water. This phenomenon, and a misunderstanding of their complete life cycle, has given rise to their Latin name *Ephemera* — living for a day — and the word ephemeral to describe the fleeting nature of existence.

Though trout feed on mayfly nymphs all year round, hunting them among the river gravels and picking off the insects dislodged by the current, like the anglers, they are especially attuned to the mayfly hatch calendar. The ascending insects, briefly trapped in the surface film, are at their most vulnerable — away from the safety and shelter of riverbed crevices, caught out in the open and silhouetted against the sky. No surprise then, as I watched, the weaving currents of the Waiau were roiled with the feeding frenzy of trout, the fish slashing and punching from beneath the surface, their jaws snapping like so many pairs of wet hands.

You'd think that with trout feeding with such ferocity no mayfly could escape the onslaught and surely the species had to be doomed. But the insects' strength is in their numbers and the sheer violent brevity of their emergence. Some of the hatches in the US have been so huge and dense, they registered on the airports' radar systems. One species, *Hexagenia limbata*, hatches

Some of the hatches in the US have been so huge and dense, they registered on the airports' radar systems.

in such numbers on the Mississippi, their total population is estimated at around 18 trillion – more than 3000 times the number of people on earth. The newly emerged insects are attracted to lights in riverside towns and descend on them like a blizzard. The local authorities use snow-clearing vehicles to sweep up in the aftermath.

Above the Waiau, the airspace was uncontrolled and the river would do most of the cleaning up, but still there was a palpable density to the air as thousands of fluttering insects streamed skywards.

Every cast produced a violent hook-up and a blistering downstream run. But, as I was stuck on the slippery boulder, unable to move or even stand up, I could not follow the fish down, and, despite the 10-lb tippet, neither could I haul them up against the muscular greenstone current. There were sunken trees down below and the fish seemed to know that, too, because each one headed directly for them.

My mayfly imitations were the size of small butterflies and I fished them barbless, and so each time, after the nature of connection with the trout changed from the series of electrifying shocks to a steady tug of war, I dropped the rod tip and let the fish come off free.

I'd pull the line in, dry the fly with Amadou and desiccant powder, and cast again, eliciting another instant take. It was like getting drunk on shots of single malt gulped in quick succession, taking in only the distilled and purest essence of it all – no fighting or netting, just the takes and the unstoppable first runs. I lost count of the number of fish I had on; it was all a blur of elation and hatch fever that makes your hands shake as if it all was happening for the first time ever.

Then the night fell and the spectacle ended as if by the flick of a light switch. The trout were gone just as instantly, and I turned on

my headtorch, slithered off the boulder and climbed up the steep rainforest bank, heading back to my camper. Pausing for one last look at the river from the swingbridge, it occurred to me that the mayflies, and the mesmerising spectacle they provide and how this attracts the predatory salmonids, was probably the very reason why I fly-fished for trout.

There are few sights surer to gladden the heart of a fly angler, and to send his or her pulse racing, than the hatching of mayflies. The duns, like miniature sailing boats, bobbing down the current lines, drying their upright wings, and the snout of trout bulging in through the surface film to intercept them. The sheen of glassy pools, backlit by a sunset, smooth but for rise rings opening like craters in the liquid metal, and the fall of spent spinners on a cold autumn afternoon, when it seems to rain bugs out of the clear watery-blue sky.

Uniquely among insects, hatching mayflies undergo not one metamorphosis but two. The first adult form emerging from the nymphal shuck on the water's surface is a dull-coloured sub-imago, or dun, which flutters off into the air and immediately seeks the shelter of riverside vegetation. After a few hours, the dun once again sheds its skin, this time to transform into a bright and shiny imago, or spinner. The mating dance, with columns of insects shimmering above the river, and the hopping upstream flights of the egg-laying females, take place next and afterwards, their life cycle completed, the mayflies — now known as spent spinners — fall back into the water, their lustre gone, their wings no longer up like sails but flat on the water, the shape of propeller blades.

Entomologists are unsure about the evolutionary logic behind this two-step transformation, but it is thought that perhaps there is too big a change from an aquatic gilled nymph to an airborne and mature adult to be accomplished in a single transition. Whatever the reason for this eccentricity, as an evolutionary design mayflies have been extraordinarily successful. They are not only present throughout the world — with some 2500 described species, over 50 of them in New Zealand — but these insects, so seemingly ephemeral that in many languages they are commonly known as 'one-day flies', have been around for the past 350 million years, and in a virtually unchanged form. Unchanged except for the size.

Gleaned only from fossil imprints in the Carpathian Mountains and dating back some 300 million years, the world's largest known mayfly, *Bojophlebia prokopi*, had a wingspan of forty-five centimetres. In the air, it would have cut the silhouette of a hawk and their prolific hatch would have been frightening. Many smaller species have been found preserved in amber, both Siberian and Baltic, their slender and fleeting beauty frozen in time, elevated to the ranks of gemstones.

Fly anglers have always gone to extraordinary effort to understand mayflies, even going as far as setting up freshwater aquaria and stocking them with mayfly nymphs collected from the stream. Some would invest in aeration pumps to recreate a moving-water environment and powerful microscopes to look up close on their charges. They would observe the metamorphosis of the insects through their stages of development, their swimming motion and the way how, just prior to hatching, a tiny bubble of air forms between the new body and the outer shuck, allowing the nymphs to be 'airlifted' to the surface.

Along the way, they would acquire an almost encyclopaedic knowledge of the insects, not only referring to them by the names of the flies that imitate them — Twilight Beauty, Kakahi Queen, or Grey Ghost — but commonly describing them by their scientific names: *Zephlebia* and *Deleatidium*, *Ameletopsis* and *Nesameletus*, *Ichthybotus* and *Oniscigaster*, or the *Coloburiscus humeralis* I saw on the Waiau. Thus they have elevated fly-fishing to a curious mix of home-grown science and a mystery school, with a mayfly as its symbol. In New Zealand, this approach was pioneered by the late Norman Marsh.

Marsh immigrated from Lancashire in 1953, settled in Invercargill, and found his angling paradise in Southland, and especially on the Clinton River along which the Milford Track was built. He worked as an electrician, did maintenance on the track, and fished every spare hour; that is, when he was not studying streamside insects.

The result of his decades-long enquiry into the lives of our river bugs is the *Trout Stream Insects of New Zealand* which has remained a bible for angler entomologists. Thanks to Marsh's popular work, you can now, as I have once, run into men lunching on a riverbank in Southland, a farmer and a roading contractor taking a break from fishing, discussing with some authority the differences between *Deleatidium myzobranchia* and *Deleatidium vernale*, talking cerci (tail), thorax and variegation of the wing patterns, all the while keeping an eye on the river to see what might alight above it. Over anglers and scientists alike, mayflies have a way of casting their special kind of magic.

'It is easy to fall under their spell,' Ken Whelan told me. 'As a species, mayflies must be a contender for the world's most elegant insect.'

Down the angling grapevine I had heard that Whelan, an Irish ecologist recognised as one of the world's foremost experts on mayflies, was visiting New Zealand and I arranged a rendezvous with him on a trout river in the Mackenzie Country.

Whelan has led a salmonid life since the age of four. 'As a child I had a severe case of polio and it was questionable if I'd ever walk again properly,' he said. 'So while other boys ran about playing soccer and rugby, I stayed with my father who worked the peat bogs, and at my own slow pace started wandering the banks of rivers and creeks. And I got absolutely besotted by flowing water and the life within and around it: the trout and salmon, and the insect communities, the entire cold-water ecosystem.'

Later in life, Whelan would also become a leading authority in restoration of freshwater fisheries for trout and salmon, their protection and management, but his signature project, and the subject of his PhD, was to re-establish mayfly species into several limestone loughs in the Irish moorlands.

'No one had ever attempted anything like that before, and you must know that in Ireland angling is huge and deadly serious, and mayflies are something of a national insect,' he said. 'I secured the use of an old fish hatchery, but I had to collect hundreds of insects in the wild and the locals became suspicious that I was poaching their mayflies for sale in a Chinese restaurant.'

Collecting insects was a precise and delicate work — stocking net atop a long fishing pole — as the females needed to be captured after they had mated but before they laid their eggs. 'I found out that mayflies are triggered into laying eggs by contact with water,' Whelan said. 'If you hold them by their folded wings and lightly touch their abdomen to the water surface they release a glue-like droplet of eggs.' Once in the water, the glue dissolves and the eggs disperse, and the invisible part of the mayfly life cycle begins among the underwater gravels and stones.

Thus one egg-laying insect at a time, Ken Whelan hand-planted and restored the mayfly populations to several lakes and eventually even the taciturn Irish anglers had forgiven his transgression, once they saw how his work benefited their sport.

'I wanted to figure out how to do it, and to prove that it could be done, and this I did,' Whelan said, 'but it's a painstaking work and it seems a much wiser course of action never to let the water quality deteriorate to the point where the mayflies are gone from the aquatic environment.'

And here's perhaps the reason why we all need to know about mayflies and their role in riverine ecosystems. Fly-fishers may idolise and revere them, and go gaga over various imitations and new tying materials, but the most important fact about mayflies is that their presence and well-being are a direct indicator of the quality of water.

'Many mayfly species are sensitive or intolerant to pollution and so by looking at their populations — numbers, diversity and distribution — you can take a quick and easy but descriptive picture of water quality in a particular river or stream,' Whelan said.

There are two main ways of assessing water quality in a river, he went on, a chemical analysis, where samples of water are tested in a laboratory, and a biological assessment which involves looking at the different macro-invertebrate species which live in the water, like the mayflies. Chemical analysis can identify specific pollutants and the conditions of the river at the time of testing, but the biological assessment shows the long-term effects of pollutants on aquatic organisms, thus giving a truer indication of the river's state.

To make such a biological assessment, ecologists like Whelan sample a fast-flowing section of a river and collect all the specimens found in the area into a mesh net. Then they count and identify the collected critters. Though all present macro-invertebrates are taken into account, the biodiversity of mayflies is particularly telling. They are abundant, well-studied and found in bodies of water throughout the world, thus providing solid baseline material for comparisons and conclusions, and because of their limited mobility and the entire life cycle spent within the short stretch of a river, their presence, numbers, or lack thereof, give a reasonably accurate representation of the health of the waterway.

But, of course, this data is subject to interpretations and, in the current economic climate, often something of an inconvenient truth. The river I would fish with Whelan was flowing straight out of the mountains and it teemed with trout and invertebrates. It could top any water-quality charts, and I for one never hesitated to drink from it. But further downstream, past a complex of industrial dairy farms, it would become a different river entirely.

'Considering your current water-quality crisis, I think New Zealand needs to pay a lot closer attention to its freshwater invertebrates, like mayflies, and the story they tell,' Whelan told me. 'It is no longer about trout fishing or preserving species of insects. It's about water and water is life, their qualities directly proportional to each other. It seems your corporate dairy farmers are still refusing to bite the bullet regarding control of phosphorus and nitrogen that go into the waterways. You really need to learn the lessons from Europe, where reductions in loadings of these two nutrients has resulted in a dramatic improvement in water quality and restoration of natural ecosystems. All that without an adverse effect on the farming economy.'

I left Whelan to his fishing. He was a boy again — wandering the riverbanks, looking under stones, enthusing about mayfly hatches — and I travelled out of the Mackenzie and down the Waitaki Valley, to visit a pioneering mayfly research project and to see just how it might help New Zealand water-quality issues.

The foothills of the Kakanui Mountains, inland from Oamaru, are a Hobbiton landscape of pastoral prosperity, cut through with pine windbreaks and bands of weathered Otekaike limestone, drained by innumerable creeks, the tendrils of the Waitaki. On one of such creeks, I met Otago University's freshwater ecologist Andreas Bruder, who was conducting an experiment to find out exactly how aquatic ecosystems function under pressure from human-induced environmental stress.

'Our main objective is to find out the threshold between land use and ecological integrity,' Bruder told me, 'to what intensity you can farm the land while maintaining its water quality, what are the levels of impact and their downstream effects.'

The site of the project, the first of its kind in the world, was also poised on the threshold: above it there are unpopulated mountains and low-density sheep farming, immediately below a brand-new dairy conversion, pharaonic in its scale and going up on the fast-forward. The experiment itself, funded by the Ministry for Primary Industries, originated as research into the effects of dicyandiamide (DCD) on aquatic ecosystems, after the international furore caused by detectable amounts of this nitrate inhibitor found in New Zealand-made infant formula. But since the dairy industry's voluntary ban on DCD, the project had evolved into a study of how various environmental stressors caused by human land activity affect the quality of water.

'We are particularly interested in how these stressors combine and to what effect,' Bruder said, showing me around the set-up, 'so we've devised a system in which we can manipulate the key individual stressors — nutrification levels, sediments, reduced flow, increased water temperatures — and see what results they have on invertebrate communities and trout.'

Though the project was cutting-edge and the world's first, it was also done in the unmistakably home-grown can-do Kiwi style, made almost entirely from parts and supplies you'd find in any hardware store. Over the scaffold skeleton there was a spaghetti of garden hoses, with tanks and multiple valves, feeding fresh water from the creek into 128 identical aquaria containing insect communities and fish. Not so different from Norman Marsh's work but on an industrial scale.

The aquaria themselves were made from microwave cake tins, and they were covered with factory-workers' hairnets to contain the wildlife. Each container and its inhabitants were subjected to a different mix of environmental stressors, simulating a scenario in a stream or a river.

'We've designed the experiment so it not only covers all possible combinations of stressors but also so it's not a lab exercise but real-life, applied ecology,' Bruder said. 'The results will have high statistical power and reality, and the same research formula can be used all over the world. We have just helped to establish a similar set-up in Germany.' Because of their population densities, the European countries face an entirely different set of water-quality issues and environmental stressors in their waterways, Bruder said, like detectable levels of antibiotics, even caffeine.

The Otago experiment was in its final stages, most of the data measured and collected, only the results to be written up, conclusions presented to the funder. As science goes, it was applied ecology at its best, robust and realistic. But would its findings be applied with the equal realism, common sense and immediacy that was required? Or would they again be subverted, buried in incomprehensible jargon and legalese, or endlessly discussed as much of the inconvenient and embarrassing truth about the state of our water? Like the facts that sixty per cent of New Zealand rivers were no longer safe for swimming, that there were outbreaks of *E. coli* deep in the water table, that the dairy effluent – an equivalent of a population exceeding 90 million people's worth of untreated sewage – was seeping into the ground and entering the country's waterways?

Bruder was stoical about this. 'We are scientists, we're good with data,' he said. 'We produce evidence, modelling and guidelines. The rest is up to the decision-makers. But our results will certainly be in the public domain for all to see. It's a part of our contract, and at the core of our scientific integrity.'

Just then we were graced with an unexpected show of mayfly magic.

Rune Knudsen, a Norwegian salmonid expert on a sabbatical in New Zealand and helping Bruder with all things fishy, had been wandering the creek bed and now he called out to us.

'Guys, you've got to come and see this.'

In the shallows of the creek, where large rocks rose above the water surface like islands, mayflies were hatching, and they were huge. Not the usual mosquito size but the length of your fingertip, and bright yellow, like the blossom of broom and gorse which inflamed the hillsides and riverbanks around us. Their nymphs did not swim up to the surface but crawled on to the dry part of the rocks and for a few moments sat there resting, yellow buds ready to burst open. Then, in a blink of an eye, they were out of their drab

We watched transfixed. In three decades of fly-fishing, hundreds of days on rivers around the country, I had never seen mayflies this big and colourful.

nymphal shucks, golden wings up like hoisted sails, still wet but fluttering in the breeze and drying fast.

We watched transfixed. In three decades of fly-fishing, hundreds of days on rivers around the country, I had never seen mayflies this big and colourful. Bruder and Knudsen were equally perplexed; we could not even identify the species. Then, ephemeral as always, the hatch was over and the golden mayfly duns vanished, camouflaged against the blossom of broom and gorse, waiting to undergo their final transformation.

'Beyond pure aesthetics, mayflies are such remarkable little animals,' Bruder's face was still lit up from the encounter. 'They are the link between algae and fish, and so for such tiny things they play a huge role in the ecosystem. In one life, they live in two worlds — water and land — and to me, they connect these two worlds. They connect a river to the landscape. When you stand on top of a mountain and look down, you see patches: forests, rivers, pastures — seemingly disconnected fragments — but when you watch mayflies, below and above the water level, you realise that it is all one system. Within it, everything is connected and every fragment is necessary.'

In New Zealand, the best and most consistent place to experience mayfly magic is in Southland, in the catchments of the Mataura, Aparima and the Waiau, especially in their middle reaches where the water is slower and sheltered with trees, the mayfly life prolific beyond belief and the sheer natural biomass of trout unlikely to be matched anywhere else. This is not really a secret; after all, the town of Gore proclaimed itself 'the brown trout capital of the world' and some of the local anglers, like my regular fishing companion and guide Brendan Shields, flatly refuse to put on nymphs because down here, the 'fly' in 'fly-fishing' is invariably a dry fly and 'nymphs' are things you carry but hope to never use.

The abundance of mayflies and trout, however, does not mean that the fishing is easy. Your casts need to be accurate, delicate, and to drift down without drag. Only then does the entomology of the *Ephemera* come into play.

One unforgettable day I was fishing the Mataura with Brendan, and Gavin Hurley, another one of the converts who stumbled into Southland nearly two decades ago, fell in love with the style of fishing here, and has been coming back every year ever since. Fishing with Gav is like being on a river with your personal clown — the entertainment is assured regardless of how the fishing goes.

But even the old trout dogs are not immune to hatch fever and none of us was prepared for what we saw as we crested a small ridge and came down to the river. The entire pool, from the bank at our feet to the opposite side against the trees, and up for maybe half a kilometre, was alive with rising trout. It was late in the season and the river word was that pods of fresh fish were moving upstream, slowly getting ready to spawn but still feeding voraciously along the way, behaving like they had never seen an artificial fly before. It looked like we had just stumbled across one such pod. This was going to be the day of days. Or was it?

I cast to the nearest fish with my first-choice CDC emerger and got an instant refusal. Several fly changes later — parachutes and hi-vis CDC duns — and the result was the same.

'Ideas?' I turned to my companions.

'Have you got a Hubert's Red?' Gav offered.

'Never heard of it.'

'Mate, if you haven't got Hubert's Reds here, you're not really fishing.'

He gave me one, a perfect imitation of a *Deleatidium*, with just enough chestnut sheen to it, and I tied it on and cast, and it didn't work either.

A river full of rising trout, three guides on the bank, half an hour of effort and not a single hook-up. I was beginning to feel more than a little despondent.

'I think they're on spent spinners,' Brendan said in his usual understated way. This would have been odd, because we could clearly see the mayflies hatching as well. Still, this was a natural conclusion, the final step in the emerger-dun-spent progression which we always used.

I fished a Rusty Spinner out of my fly box, much like the Hubert's but with CDC wings out flat and . . . it was as if the floodgates of plenty opened for us. As it's so often the case in Southland, breaking the code was not about match-the-hatch choice of colour or size, but in precise imitation of the rise form.

I was fishing with my favourite Opti Stream 3 wt, and so it was rod tip-to-the-knuckle kind of action from the moment of the take. By then, Gav was already in the water, casting, and Brendan was changing his fly. For the next hour and a half, we hooked fish after fish, taking turns at the point, leading each trout downstream so as not to disturb the rest of the pod and, still, there were moments we all had a fish on at the same time.

Then, again, as if a switch has been flipped, the 'hatch' was over, and river surface gone instantly quiet. By then we were nearly at the head of the pool, having caught just about every fish we cast to.

'Speight's o'clock,' Gav declared, shaking off his net. Unlike trout, he had always been delightfully predictable and consistent in his taste.

For a fly angler, a Southland hatch or a spinner fall — its intensity, magnitude, sheer beauty and the excitement of fishing it — can be a life-changing experience. Whatever else may be happening on the water, I'm forever on the lookout for the tiny ballerinas with fairy wings and their peculiar kind of magic.

A glimpse into the world of mayflies, however — if you're receptive to it — offers a lot bigger picture than just what to tie on at the end of your tippet, and this is how and why I found myself in the roomy elevator at the Canterbury Museum in Christchurch, which has secret back doors built into it. Swiping his magnetic pass through a card reader, Terry Hitchings opened them for me, leading the way into a part of the museum never seen by the public. The collections rooms: temperature-controlled vaults lit by strips of fluorescent lights, floor-to-ceiling aisles of books. Framed sheets of insects, each bug pinned and carefully labelled, cabinets of drawers with perforated bottoms, each hole containing a glass vial with a small creature in preserving liquid. A repository of academic knowledge, this particular floor devoted entirely to entomology, and in its centre, three men bent over microscopes looking for glimpses of the unknown, unseen or undescribed.

'There is no money in mayflies,' Terry laughed. 'Most of entomological research in New Zealand is driven by the needs of agriculture. Mayflies are not a pest but they have no economic value either so we are all labourers of love here.'

Terry was a retired physics and chemistry teacher, a man with a sharp and lively mind who had voluntarily devoted his golden years to the study and description of the country's mayflies because, as he said, after many years of fly-fishing he found invertebrates far more interesting.

I immediately saw him as one of those nineteenth-century amateur entomologists, out in the field in khaki shorts and with a butterfly net, collecting specimens, bringing his catches home to lucubrate over them under the microscope, writing up detailed descriptions, fuelled by pure curiosity and infinite wonder. And, as we talked, these initial impressions were only strengthened.

'Places like the museum are the last bastions of blue-sky science, a quest for knowledge and understanding that is driven by curiosity rather than corporate agendas,' Terry said. 'The information we collect here has a lot of aesthetic value and reason but that's what gets me out of bed at six-thirty in the morning, into the field and back into the lab. I just love the discipline of following the rules of good science: to observe not jumping to conclusions, to be objective about the evidence, not bending it to suit a preferred outcome.'

Clearly an attractive proposition because Terry's son Tim, a Christchurch doctor, was now also helping with the research at the museum, taking time off from a busy medical practice to delve into the world of tiny ballerinas with fairy wings.

Beyond the inroads made by the fly-fishers, how much do we really know about New Zealand mayflies, I asked. Where are we at in our enquiry into the *Ephemera*?

'It's interesting to note that, unlike most of the world, New Zealand has no stillwater mayflies,' Terry said. 'No one has conclusively answered why it is so, but I'd offer that it's because, in geological terms, our lakes are still very young so no species of mayflies has evolved to colonise their littoral zones.

'As for diversity, North Island forest streams seem to have most of it, though keep in mind that our knowledge of mayfly distribution depends more on where people have collected rather than where mayflies are most numerous or diverse,' he went on. 'What we know is far from complete. In fact, what we have are more fragments of the puzzle than the whole picture of it.'

No doubt the father-and-son team would continue to add new pieces to this understanding, if for no other reason than because, as Terry put it, science is as selfish as fly-fishing: there is an enormous satisfaction to be derived from learning and discovery. But there is also a greater wisdom to be found in the fleeting flutter of a mayfly and its fate.

'Consider that the so seemingly fragile and short-lived mayfly has survived in a virtually unchanged form for the past 350 million years, until it encountered the wonders of the Industrial Revolution and now the industrialised dairy farming,' Terry Hitchings said. 'That alone should give us a reason to pause and rethink. Every time we lose a species our lives become poorer. And as we lose them, the earth becomes a more lonely place in which to live.

'Yet so often, in conservation alarmism, we hear that we now have to take radical measures to save the planet,' he went on, 'but, like the aspects of mayfly science, the issue is also a lot more selfish than that. The planet is not endangered by human activity. It has been around for billions of years and it will continue to survive. What is endangered by human activity are human beings. What we so urgently need to do now is not about "saving the planet" but about saving ourselves and the quality of our life with this planet.'

We may be fascinated with the mayflies and their fleeting life cycles, Terry suggested, but on a larger scale of things, our own existence here and its quality is as delicate as that of a mayfly, and just as ephemeral.

chapter 9

WE WERE PADDLING THE WESTERN SHORELINE of Lake Te Anau, in two single sea kayaks, with ten days of food and firewater in the spacious bulkheads, fly rods at hand in rod holders, nets tucked under the back bungee cords and within easy reach. The coastline is like no other: rocky and steep, with near-vertical walls rising above for hundreds of metres, covered with densely woven trees and bushes, a kind of hanging forest. As there is almost no soil, the trees cling precariously to the rock and to each other. When they become saturated with rain, strips of forest tear down and peel off like wet wallpaper, a uniquely Fiordland phenomenon known as 'tree avalanches'. Some of the avalanche paths are the size of small airport runways, an eerie sight and concept when your kayak is stealthily slicing across the glassy lake water directly below them.

Geologists tell us that Fiordland's dramatic landscape continues below the sea and lake levels — both lakes Te Anau and Manapouri are said to be over 400 metres deep — but to a fly angler the most interesting part is where the green rock walls and the lake waters meet. There, a few metres from the wall, often closer, a tidemark-like feed lane forms — part foam and part leaves but clearly part insects too because good-sized trout cruise these lanes and they are undisturbed and unsuspecting, and eagerly looking at dry flies.

Sure, a kayak is no SUP and somewhat awkward to sight-fish from — being so low in the water severely restricts your visibility — but since you can get really close to these fish, the visibility is not a problem and, besides, travelling by a sea kayak offers both stealth and beautiful self-containment, and you can really cover a lot of distance if you put your muscles to it.

The many rivers entering the fiords from the west are of course a trout world unto themselves, some of the best and wildest New Zealand has to offer, and no one I can think of has fished them more than Dean Bell. He was, in fact, to be on this trip, or rather to lead it, but a string of health issues put him out of action, the last of which was a sprained ankle just days before we were supposed to meet. With much regret, we had to cancel every single one of our trout dates together.

'Just not meant to happen,' he texted. 'I'll see you again in winter. I don't have a single day free between now and the end of the season.'

And so we went without him.

There is a lost world *feeling to this place, and not just because its topography echoes the . . . Venezuelan 'islands in time' that inspired Arthur Conan Doyle's classic. It was a fitting place to rediscover an extinct species.*

Fishing or not, Fiordland never gets old. I've been coming here for years, mainly to fish and hike but also to adventure deeper and further afield in what still is the largest undisturbed piece of wilderness in this country. Once we did the second-ever ascent of the Kaipo Wall, a 1300-metre Yosemite-like feature north of Milford Sound, another time we sea-kayaked around Doubtful Sound, a ten-day jaunt at the time when it was still an expedition, not a backpacking day trip. But perhaps the most memorable of all the outings were several visits into the Murchison Mountains, to find the elusive takahe, up from and beyond the very shoreline we were paddling now.

The takahe, like a pukeko but the size of a turkey, is a kind of New Zealand equivalent of the dodo. Except that, while the dodo did not just go extinct but became the very symbol of extinction, the takahe — also considered gone forever — was found again alive and well here in the Murchison Mountains, rediscovered and captured with a net by an Invercargill doctor and amateur naturalist Geoffrey Orbell. It became the bird that came back from the dead, not just a sign of hope but a form of ecological resurrection as well.

The Murchisons, designated a Special Area off limits to the public, stand on the western side of Lake Te Anau like a tall fortress — back against the spine of the Main Divide, three flanks guarded by deep fiords. From the air they resemble an archipelago of bald islands rising from the rainforest: snow-white against dark green, serrated contours chiselled by ice-age glaciers, their rock faces and couloirs never scaled by climbers. There is a *lost world* feeling to this place, and not just because its topography echoes the shapes of *tepuis*, the Venezuelan 'islands in time' that inspired Arthur Conan Doyle's classic. It was a fitting place to rediscover an extinct species.

We had flown in one summer evening and set up a camp on the lip of a glacial cirque that dropped down to McKenzie Burn, and we woke up in winter, after the overnight storm had dumped half a metre of snow on the mountains. And yet, a short distance from the camp, using radio transceivers to locate them, we found a pair of adult takahe, plodding around in the snow.

Up close their feathers had the iridescence of a polished paua shell, their beaks marbled with shades of red, but from a distance the birds were inky blue, though the carmine beaks were a giveaway, attracting the eye like a light. For a timeless moment we watched them, but then with a couple of quick steps, both birds vanished under the tussocks, into the grassy thicket riddled with their tunnel-like trails and now covered by snow. We would not see them again, but their image lingered in my mind like a memory afterburn. This was my private 'Doc Orbell' moment, rediscovering for myself the takahe in the wild.

Later on the same mission, I was fortunate to encounter the man himself and that was even more unforgettable. 'Doc' Orbell was a big man with wide shoulders and, when I met him in his Central Otago home, his voice seemed a little loud and harsh until you noticed his hearing aid. His chihuahua nipped at my heels as he led me to a sunny, glassed-in verandah and sat me down next to a fruiting lemon tree.

'Good thing you got me when you did,' he said. 'I'll be away in Australia for the next couple of months.' A sensible thing to do with the winter upon us, I agreed. Would he be visiting his family? That too, he said, but mainly it will be a 4WD expedition around the northern Queensland national parks.

Geoffrey Orbell was ninety. The pipe on which he marked the size of the takahe footprints was long gone — he gave up smoking forty years ago — and, apart from a few metres of footage in his son-in-law's possession, he didn't know what had become of his famous takahe film. When I asked about the events of 1948, he seemed tired of launching into another repetitive recollection. He gave me a printed account. 'It's all in there,' he said.

I wondered if, like Sir Edmund Hillary, this larger-than-life character felt typecast and branded for life with only one of his achievements. That would be unfortunate, because there clearly was much more to Doc Orbell than takahe.

He had been a lifelong GP who put himself through medical school by trapping rabbits. 'Back then, if you got thirty or forty skins a week, you were into good money,' he told me. In 1952, he surveyed and mapped what must have been the last chunk of true wilderness in the country: the Murchison Mountains, takahe country.

'When we started, there was only a contour of the coast,' he recalled. 'The interior was all labelled "UNEXPLORED". We did the eastern side and a Canterbury crowd did the west. When we put the two maps together there was no room for the Chester Burn; we had an overlap of two miles.' Only later, a coastal survey showed the South Island to be two miles wider than previously thought.

For twelve years, during the red deer plague in Fiordland, Orbell was a government hunter. He was shooting so much that frequently his ears bled from the noise of rifle fire.

In his life he had been a boatbuilder and a Scout leader, and he had visited sixty-one countries. The manuscripts recounting his adventures — written as a family record — could fill a large suitcase. 'I've had a busy life,' he said, nodding at the stack.

He may have tired of takahe, but you only needed to tickle his curiosity — to hint at a mystery or point at a remote place on a map — and the young Geoffrey who was once obsessed with a supposedly extinct bird, and with the wilderness at large, came forward to meet you.

'You see, Captain Cook named things after what he saw there,' he told me, warming to a new topic. 'Cormorant Cove after a cormorant, Duck Cove after a duck, Dusky Sound after dusk, Woodhen Cove after a weka. But what about Goose Cove? There were no geese in New Zealand back then. I've been to this place — Five Fingers Peninsula, near Resolution Island. I reckon a small bush moa in tall grass could, from a distance, look just like a goose.'

This thought led him to some impromptu research and . . . a disappointment. It turned out that Cook named the cove after the last five of the geese that he had brought from England and released in Dusky Sound. Orbell was unfazed. There was adventure in such homework, in sifting through records and folklore, disentangling facts from rumours, finding a goal for another expedition. Once in a while you may take on a myth and prove it true.

'If only I was younger, I'd still love to have another good look around there anyway,' he smiled.

And I'm sure he'd carry a net. Just in case.

Why am I telling you all this? Because fly-fishing travels, at their best and if we are receptive, can take us beyond themselves, into the bigger-picture, broader conclusions and more universal truths. They can take us places and enable us to meet people that often have nothing to do with trout or fishing and yet inspire us and remain in our memories long after images of trout have faded away.

For me, Doc Orbell — who is no longer with us — was one of these people, and my entire takahe encounter was originally inspired by a chance riverside meeting with an angler who also happened to work on the takahe conservation team. If I didn't get into a conversation about the *Coloburiscus humeralis* with the guy — borrowed his flies even as the first time around I didn't have anything big enough — I might have only known about Doc Orbell and his birds from the glossed-over and cliched accounts in the nation's common history and never by direct experience. And I wouldn't even know what I'd missed out on.

Back along the Te Anau's western coastline, we camped, and fished, and explored the fiords and the rivers that enter them until our food and booze were running low. We missed Dean Bell, and his dry sense of humour, and at beach campfires we wondered about the mysteries of the fiords, about Doc Orbell and how amazing it must have been to be the first-ever European explorer here. I even had a pipe for the occasion but, times being what they are, it was not filled with tobacco but its substitute: dry rose petals, and organic at that.

When it was time to go back we rose well before dawn as the lake crossings are never to be taken lightly. Later in the day, big swells often build up down each of the fiords and where they collide at right angles, a vicious cross-chop develops, no place for a kayak. But at this cold and early hour, as our boats skimmed across the glassy lake, the water surface was so still the islands seemed to be floating above it like a mirage, perfect green discs against metallic silver of the lake, the land and its reflection merged into one.

Above the water and the thin fog behind us, the Murchison Mountains hovered like the true 'lost world' that they are.

We had barely got out of the car when Jennifer pointed out to the river and said: 'There, a fish just rose! There! Another one! See it?'

How could I have not? When you spend a large part of your life walking rivers and lake shores, staring into the water both moving and still in search of feeding fish, when even at night when you

close your eyes you see the afterburn of river currents replaying against the back of your eyelids, the sight of rising trout attracts your vision like red flashing neons. And these fish, porpoising to intercept tiny mayflies hatching through the surface of the Fryingpan River, were indeed flashing red, their camouflage cued off the brick-red basalt rocks which framed the river and studded its bottom.

Knowing just how short-lived a hatch can be, we were in the water in no time, taking a side of the river each. I put on a generic CDC dun and promptly caught my first Colorado trout, a brown of not quite two pounds but glowing bright with those red-rock markings. As I was admiring it in the net, Jen's girlish scream announced she was hooked up too. I glanced upstream and saw an untold number of fish rising almost continuously. This Colorado fishing was too easy, I thought. Casting with our New Zealand-style accuracy and finesse we'd clean the river up, leave no fish unhooked.

Well, it was as if I jinxed the fishing with this very thought. After those first instant couple of fish the action had suddenly died off. There were trout rising all around us like before, not at all spooking even if some of them were too close to even cast to, and yet they all completely ignored our flies. I changed and changed, going through my tried and tested mayfly patterns and none would elicit even a half-hearted look.

It was early May, in the Colorado high country the beginning of northern-hemisphere spring. With the New Zealand trout year about to enter its annual lowest point, and with my commitments fulfilled and finished, all I could think of was being back with Jennifer. She had promised to show me her favourite trout streams and for both of us that seemed a good enough excuse. I placed Maya back with her two younger Airedale sisters and the care of their owners – she couldn't wait to be back with them all – and in no time at all I was on the plane to Murica, to Jennifer, and my introduction to Colorado trout.

That first day was grey and cold, perfect for dry-fly action as the nasty weather tends to slow down the emergence of mayflies, keeping them longer in and on the surface before they can hatch, dry and flutter off to safety. The rise wasn't stopping anytime soon, which presently only fuelled my frustration. To be surrounded by rising trout yet unable to hook up no matter what you do is torture by fly-fishing. You begin to wonder how come the journey from elation to despair could be a matter of only a few casts, and even more so, how can you turn this sad situation around.

If good things can come out of frustration, this was one of those times. About to give up with the lack of further options, and with the trout rising even more feverishly than before, I suddenly remembered my 'Welcome to Colorado' gift fly box from Jennifer's father, Brit, who had fished these waters for more decades than he'd like to admit.

His flies were tiny, way smaller than anything I'd ever used, mid-20s and even finer, but all exquisitely tied. Out of the entire selection, one pattern instantly stood out for me, the same way those flashing red trout did earlier. It was a shuttlecock emerger, much like what we use in Southland but about half the size and with a white wing for better visibility on the water. Not really a close imitation of the naturals but near enough in size.

The first cast and an extended drift elicited a couple of close inspections, the second cast resulted in a solid take. I dried the fly with Loon dust, recast, and hooked up again. We were back in the game, the riddle solved.

'Jen, they're taking your old man's Blue-Winged Olives, about the size of a sandfly,' I called out. 'Come and get one.' And she did.

It was the only fly we used the rest of the day. For the next few hours, until the hatch ended abruptly at around four o'clock, we were side by side in every fly-fisher's promised land. The rise was as intense as anything I'd seen on the Mataura, and a lot longer, and though the fish were small they took eagerly, and fought valiantly, and they dazzled with their red-gold markings. We had this stretch of river all to ourselves too, something which, I was later to learn, was the rarest of things around here.

'This must be the most beautiful trout water I've ever seen,' Jennifer on the edge of Kahurangi National Park.

No shortage of big days. The more effort and mileage you put in, the better the fishing gets, maybe not always in pounds and inches of trout but certainly in decibels of silence and solitude.

Through the heart of Colorado's high country flow the iconic gold-medal trout rivers of the American West, and Jennifer's home waters — the Fryingpan (above) and the Roaring Fork (below) — renowned for year-round hatches and thousands of fish per mile.

In Colorado, private ownership of riverbanks limits public access to select locations (above) and makes float fishing (middle right) a preferred option. The fish often cue their camouflage off the red basalt rock (middle left) and in the alpine zone, above 3,000 metres, trout lakes can remain frozen well into summer.

Guiding for sighted trout in New Zealand is a dark art combining hard work and magic, knowledge and intuition, forever trying to find undisturbed water and bridging the gap between what the anglers can do and what needs to be done.

Snowstorms or sunshine, the guide's show must go on, its ultimate goal a collection of obligatory grip 'n' grins.

The phenomenal and unexpected return of sockeye salmon from presumed near extinction (above) bodes well for the future of fly-fishing in the Mackenzie Country (middle.) Though the sockeye themselves are not a game fish species, their eggs and juveniles are a major food source making the local rainbow and brown trout (bottom) grow spectacularly large.

There is no better place in New Zealand to experience the mayfly magic than on the lowland rivers of Southland where huge biomasses of trout and insects collide to produce unforgettable hatches and dry-fly action. Most local mayflies are small (#16–18) and drab but with luck you may witness the emergence of the rare Ameletopsis perscitus *which are about the size of baby birds.*

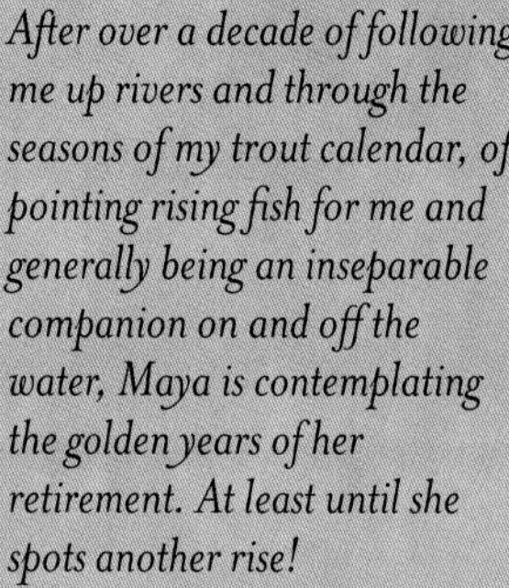

After over a decade of following me up rivers and through the seasons of my trout calendar, of pointing rising fish for me and generally being an inseparable companion on and off the water, Maya is contemplating the golden years of her retirement. At least until she spots another rise!

After the hatch, we sat on the rocky bank, warming ourselves with the sips of Laphroaig, as intense as the experience we'd just had.

'Best day ever!' Jen beamed our daily mantra.

'For my first time fishing in Colorado, this wasn't half bad,' I teased her.

She rolled her eyes and said: 'You ain't seen nothin' yet.'

Colorado, named after the mighty 2330-kilometre-long Rio Colorado river, is a land of big mountains, aspen and conifer forests, and high plateaus, most of which despite being urbanised the American way, remain remarkably wild. Black bears bumble through suburban neighbourhoods raiding fruit trees and getting high on overripe apples, deer and elk seem unafraid of humans, browsing in the front yards, there are seasonal closures of popular trails to prevent mountain lion attacks on people. Draining this land is a huge number of high-country lakes, brooks, creeks and streams combining into larger rivers and, since all of Colorado lies more than 1000 metres above sea level, the water is always cold, making it the perfect habitat for four species of trout: brown, rainbow, brook and the native cutthroat, as well as numerous other species of freshwater game fish.

These are the hallowed trout waters of the American Southwest: the Fryingpan, Roaring Fork, the Eagle and the Crystal, South Platte, Arkansas, Gunnison, and of course the Upper Colorado whose creek-like nature gives no clue that further downstream it will become the river that shapes the Grand Canyon.

At first glance, most fly-fishing done in Colorado seems fairly crude, accomplished largely with Thingamabobber indicators — plastic bubbles in varying sizes and colours — supporting double or triple nymph rigs and a great deal of split shot. Indeed, a saying here goes that 'the difference between a good Colorado angler and a great one can be as little as one split shot'. And if you said 'there can't be much to this greatness then' I could not agree with you more.

Yet beyond this 'must catch fish no matter what' approach so often adopted by the guides — and you see their clients casting those super-heavy rigs as if they were throwing grenades into the water — Colorado has some of the best dry-fly fishing you'll find anywhere, with dependable hatches all plotted out into seasonal charts.

During my previous visit, at the coldest time of the northern winter, Jennifer took me for a drive-by of the Fryingpan, and though we did not fish then, we saw plenty of fish rising to midges, all that while there was more than a foot of snow on the banks and the temperature nipped hard at around minus 20 degrees Celsius. (The season is open all year here and the non-resident state fishing licence is only US$66.)

The Blue-Winged Olives (BWOs) emergence we stumbled into was the first of the spring hatches and it was to be followed by spectacular daytime caddis action, and — after the snow run-off in May–June — the fabled salmonfly hatch, a two-inch (5-cm) long stonefly that is said to drive trout into a feeding hysteria. Then came the hatches of Golden Stoneflies, Yellow Sallies and the giant mayflies known as green drakes (about an inch long), followed by pale morning duns (PMDs) and summer trico spinnerfall (in sizes #22–26). There were the red quills of August until mid-September, then it was back to the autumn BWOs and winter midges, all in all a beautifully cyclical dry-fly year, varied and visual, one that would have me happily forgo any nymphing altogether.

But, for now, all that was yet to come. After a few more BWO days and an epic midday hatch of grey caddis where the insects rose through the air in thick upstream waves and you could catch every fish that was rising, the temps shot into the mid-twenties, and alpine snowfields released and the rivers began to flow high and dirty with snow run-off — *muy colorado* (very coloured) as the local Hispanics would put it. Since Colorado is especially known for its bottom-release tailwaters, like the Fryingpan, there are always clear-water options, even at the height of the six-week run-off, but Jennifer wanted the change of pace and style and came up with a secret plan. In New Zealand, I had shown her some of my most favourite trout places and now she wanted to do the same on her home waters.

'The run-off tends to concentrate people at the tailwaters to the point it's hard to find a place to fish, or even park, so let's go look for some brook trout in the alpine,' she said. 'The fish aren't big, but it's awful pretty up high and we won't see a soul.'

We drove up a mountain road cutting through groves of aspen until the first deep snowdrift barred our way. We hiked on, to the trailhead at the end of the road and over a high ridge and down into a picturesque alpine valley with a small stream babbling and snaking along its bottom. There were brook trout in every pool and riffle and they behaved like they had never seen a fly.

'Look at it,' Jen said, as she netted another fish for me. 'Isn't it beautiful? Like a little gem you find in the mountains.'

And I thought, 'My words, exactly.'

'I'd much rather fish here than down in the valley,' she went on. 'It's all public land up here, you can go and fish wherever you like and no one can tell you that you can't, or come out at you with a gun.'

This is perhaps the greatest shock to a visiting New Zealand angler, one used to Kiwi ways, attitudes and river etiquette, so if I sketched a somewhat overly idyllic Colorado trout dream for you let me offer a correction. You'll be driving along postcard-pretty trout rivers, seeing the perfect pools and riffles, bends and banks, watching the insects flutter above the water and getting excited about the prospects of more dry-fly magic, when it suddenly hits you that most of the water you see is locked up and out of bounds, available only to its owners and their guests, posted with unequivocal 'No Trespassing' signs.

According to the Colorado state law, the property owner has the exclusive title not just to the riverbank but also to the river bottom halfway across its width. It seems a part of the American way to want to own things and this includes rivers, trout and fly-fishing so a trout dream here involves owning a stretch of riverside property which you can fish at your leisure and to the exclusion of everyone else.

This is further enforced by another piece of legislature, commonly known as the 'Make my day' law — the name adapted from the *Dirty Harry* movies — which allows you to legally defend your property with firearms, and you know how much the 'Muricans' love their guns. There is a story told here about a sheriff pulling over an old lady on the side of the highway and she had a .38 in her handbag, a .45 in the glove compartment and a pump-action behind the seat.

'What are you afraid of, ma'am?' the sheriff asked.

'Nothin',' she replied.

Although most of the riverbanks are privately owned, the water is not, which explains the astonishing popularity of float fishing in Colorado. A drift boat — either an inflatable or a McKenzie dory — makes all trout water accessible to anyone as long as they don't park up or anchor and only fish while passing through. Not an ideal solution but a workable one. Considering it all made me realise just how fortunate we are in New Zealand to have such unrestricted access to almost all of our trout waters, something that, after experiencing America, I'll never again take for granted.

Trout and fly-fishing are a huge thing in Colorado. There are fly shops in every town and over a hundred guides in the Roaring Fork valley alone, though most are on-demand casuals. Despite the restrictions imposed by private property, there are enough public rivers and lakes here to never fish the same water twice for months if not years.

Jennifer was already planning another hike for us to the high-country cutthroat lakes, once more snowmelt makes the mountain roads passable again. Meantime, we Spey-fished barbless streamers between the hatches, and I for one could not wait for those Salmonflies and Green Drakes to come out. They were only days away now.

Over the past few years I've been getting increasingly interested in double-handed Spey fishing, something that, until very recently, has been almost unknown or at least rarely practised in New Zealand. It has been a stop-and-start progression for me — plenty of casting practice but not a lot of real-life application — and it was only after spending many days fishing with Jennifer's father Brit, especially on a big river like the Colorado, that the theory and practice began to coalesce into a useable and consistent skill.

At the tender age of his early seventies, Brit injured his right shoulder hitting a tree while skiing powder in the glades and this somewhat handicapped his ability to cast single-handed rods; in fact, to fish at all. He got around this by converting to Scandi-style Spey casting, using his right hand to guide and direct the rod and letting the left — or the under hand — to power the cast. He developed this to such a level of finesse that, with super-light double handers in the 4 — 6-wt range, he could fish to rising fish with an enviable accuracy and lightness of touch. He also helped me to disentangle some of the finer points of Spey line management — how to coil all those metres and metres of stripped fly line so the river currents don't pull it away and so it doesn't bird-nest around the reel and the long handle.

The most immediate thing you notice when you first pick up a double-handed Spey rod is its latent power and potential. It may feel like a vault pole — long and clumsy — and you may question its practical use in a country renowned for sight-fishing, but flex that tip and let the line fly, and there, without any effort or tuition at all, you've just about doubled the distance of your longest cast ever.

With that comes a sudden realisation that your journey as a fly angler has just acquired a parallel evolution, as if you've discovered fly-fishing all anew. And so you vow to learn Spey casting no matter what it takes, not just because it'll open up new waters until now beyond your reach, or get you more and perhaps bigger fish, but also because Spey casting, fish or not, can be such a consuming and fun thing to indulge in that you begin to wonder why they have not made it illegal yet.

At first I thought it was just me, being a bit of a fly-fishing poet and a sucker for new things to learn, the harder the better. But then I noticed this was something of a universal pattern, occurring whenever an angler, no matter how accomplished in the arts of trout hunting, picked up a Spey rod for the first time. Most recently, this was Murray Knowles, one of the country's original fishing guides, a man with untold backcountry mileage now retired after over forty years of 'work'. Murray came visiting and caught me playing with my 6-wt, 12-foot 2-inch LOOP Spey.

'Have a go,' I said, and he hefted the rod in both hands and shook it until the tip quivered with eagerness and purpose. Murray's face lit up.

'This would be great on the Waiau,' he said, 'and the Clutha. And . . . and . . .' In fact, once we got brainstorming, there seemed to be no shortage of big-river places where outside the traditional trout-hunting season, a long light Spey rod would be *the* tool of choice.

Over the past two winters, I've been making quiet inroads into the double-handed Spey casting, and I tell you now, it has not been an easy journey. Beyond the initial impressions of power and potential Spey seems overwhelmingly complex. There are at least three distinct styles — traditional, Scandi and Skagit — half a dozen must-have casts and just as many variations, a multitude of lines and sink tips. All of this is relatively easy to grasp as concepts, and it makes perfect sense, until you get to the river and try to use it! There, you give it your best shot, oh so educated through much reading and instructional videos, and the line comes off the water

. . . you give it your best shot, . . . and the line comes off the water with a long sickening slurp, whacks you in the back of the head, then collides with itself and lands in a heap, . . .

with a long sickening slurp, whacks you in the back of the head, then collides with itself and lands in a heap, and the only thing you're actually happy about is that, mindful of compassionate advice, you've put a piece of yarn on the end of the line, not a big weighted streamer. Otherwise you'd be on your way to the medical centre to remove barbed hardware from your anatomy.

This, of course, happens repeatedly no matter what you do, until you feel like throwing the whole outfit into the river and be done with it, and you would, only that the rig costs the equivalent of your kid's car, plus, well, you've committed to taming the thing for better or worse. Especially the worse.

To get around these initial frustrations, some novice Spey anglers even put together cheat cards which tell them which casts to use when. For example: river right + downstream wind = Double Spey or Snake Roll. All these achieve is to confuse you even further because real life does not fit into neat mathematical equations. The point is, Spey is a bit like art or Zen: you can't really understand it. You can only get it by doing, by putting in river time and developing the touch, and in this any understanding is secondary and peripheral, more an explanation of what you experience rather than a recipe for mastery.

Learning Spey happens in a series of 'aha!' moments which come in their own time, and with each of those the complexity drops away a notch until what is left is simple and natural. In this progression, thrashing water, getting tangled and frustrated is the inevitable first step. If you persevere, good things can follow: fluidity and ease, confidence and consistency, maybe even a little bit of Spey magic.

I do not profess any kind of expertise in Spey casting as yet, but I have got through the hardest part of the journey, one during which it is all too easy to give up in the face of complexity and confusion. So let me offer some fundamental ideas and revelations that came my way as they are not obvious in any study material or instructional DVDs. Once you get these, and I mean not just cerebrally but by doing, you'll see that Spey casting is as uncomplicated as it is natural. You still need to travel the entire Spey road yourself as there are no short cuts worth taking, but hopefully these pointers will dispel some of the complexity and serve as road signs and confirmations that you haven't in fact got lost along the way.

All of Spey is essentially a roll cast, always the same; the complexity and the multitude of 'different' casts — Single and Double Spey, Snake Roll, C Spey, Snap T, Snap Z and others — come from the how and where we reposition the line prior to that roll cast.

The key thing in all this repositioning is the 'line stick' — the surface tension of water against the line. Unlike in normal overhead casting, in Spey you don't have a backcast and the line stick is all there is to work with. You can hack an overhead cast, as so often performed by the exponents of the 'carpet beater school of fly-casting' where a solution to any and all problems is to apply more power, but you can't hack a Spey cast. If you cannot feel the line stick, and there are degrees of subtleties to that, your cast is just not going to go anywhere.

Most of the Spey casting is accomplished with body movements — weight shift and rotation — and arms and hands move relatively little, though with precision and timing. This is to say that if you just try to whack out the cast with your hands alone it will not go very far or collapse entirely, and the harder you try the worse it'll go. It is the body movement, of which the rod is but an extension, that makes Spey casting so elegant and effortless.

Touch and timing are everything. In a way, Spey casting connects you to the water because there is no other way to make the casts work. This in turn transfers well into your standard fishing — the mending and line control. Many anglers I see and work with appear disconnected from the water. They slap the line down and slurp it off the surface, their applied power is disproportionate to the distances they try to reach, the mending is erratic and mistimed, line control random. Their intentions, actions and results seem totally at odds with one another; if they drove the way they fish they'd lose their licence on the spot. On the river, of course, all this compounds into disturbed water and spooked fish. Spey casting has a way of fixing all that as it forces upon you precise touch and timing. So whether you aspire to fish double-handed rods or not, Spey is well worth learning for this one reason alone.

And by the way: Spey is more a style of casting than gear. You can do all the Spey casts with a single-handed rod, though some may not be practical. But learning the basics of Spey casting this way is a viable option. You may then find that you seamlessly adopt elements of Spey into your sight-fishing situations. For example, a little snake roll is an excellent and stealthy way to pick the line off the water while fishing a dry fly.

The hardest thing in Spey casting is the placement of the *anchor* — the part of line, and at more advanced level just the leader which touches the water — because how and where you place that anchor determines where you can cast. Harder still is any kind of consistency in this. You will get some good casts, when the line shooting out wants to rip the rod out of your hands, and others that just flop like a heap of spaghetti. But even if you get one or two good casts it means you can do it! Consistency comes only from time and mileage on the water.

Beyond the touch and timing, much of the confusion in Spey casting comes from which cast to use in what situation. This at first can be a real mind-twister, but again I suggest you forget those cheat cards. It's simple, really. Your first priority is to always — always! — keep the line and fly downwind of yourself. This simplifies the choice of casts by half. The other factor in choosing the cast is the direction of the current and which side of you the line ends up after the drift. Play with your options a little and you soon realise that, for any given situation there is only a couple of casts that would work and you can use either of those.

A true game changer here is learning to swap hands on the rod and be able to cast on both sides of your body. So, for example, if Single Spey is your strong cast and you're using it on one side of the river, when you cross and fish from the other bank the cast may not work any more, unless you swap hands. Learning to cast with either hand on top is a lot easier than say learning to cast single-handed with your non-dominant hand, and it doubles your options for any fishing situation.

Finally, learn one cast at a time, on both sides. Cerebral overload is a constant danger while learning the Spey so break it down into manageable chunks. To begin with, practising on still water is also a good idea as you're not limited by directions of the current. And, as in all casting, don't try to go for distance. Learn the proper form and let the distance come in its own good time. Many faults and bad habits are the result of trying to cast too far too early: the old 'carpet beater' approach again.

We can't really stalk trout with a Spey rod so this style of fishing will always remain secondary in New Zealand, but one thing's for sure, we are about to see a lot more Spey in this country, in places like the Tongariro, Clutha and Waiau, the Canterbury salmon and sea-run rivers, in fact wherever there is big water and fishing with streamers. For the first time ever, a full range of highest quality gear is available locally and, even more important, some top-notch tuition. LOOP NZ is now running regular double-handed Spey workshops in Turangi and Rakaia, and Klaus Frimor — one of the world's best casters — will be the teacher. I've already signed up.

A while ago, a good friend of mine and a river companion got his new Spey rod and took it out to our home river for a test drive. Since he was born into a family of Scottish salmon fanatics he can Spey cast well and far, but this outing was for nothing more than to get to know the rod and the feel of it. Still, he put on his favourite streamer and got into the swing of things. A few casts later he hooked up with THE fish.

'It was the biggest rainbow I've ever had on,' he would later say, 'a huge wild thing, more like a steelhead, easily into double figures.' He had the fish at his feet before it tore off for one more run and pinged him off in the swift and muscular current of the Clutha. I had fished that spot many times over the years, though even with a shooting-head line it was too far to reach the trough against the far bank where the fish was hooked. But with a Spey it would be a different game. So guess where I'll be taking my double-handed rods in winter.

chapter 10

THE MATAURA, unquestionably one of the best trout rivers on the planet and a dry-fly fisher's dream come true, is not especially renowned for trophy fish — or, at least, though they are there you never see them out in the open — so it was something of a once-in-a-decade surprise to find one of those giants on the lip of a large pool, slurping dries with not a care in the world. He was moving freely side to side, examining every passing insect, either taking or refusing but always looking, and we could watch this heart-stopping spectacle while hiding in the trees on the high bank above him.

Big though he was — the biggest fish I'd ever seen in this river — the trout was a 'sitter'. We could cast into the shallow riffle well above him so he would never see the actual cast or be disturbed by it. Even with a modicum of skills, the fish should see the fly first, and take it or not, but not be easily scared off, which could give us options for fly changes if needed.

Other than highly elevated heart rates in all three of us, there was only one problem: one of the gentlemen with me, whose turn it was, had never fly-fished before. He was apparently handy with a bait rod, but this was his first ever day on the fly. A former high-level cricketer, he had good motor skills and coordination and, all credit to him, we had already eked out his first ever trout on the fly, a couple of pools below, in the fast shallow riffle against a hedge-like bank, even though it took some twenty casting attempts to get the fly where the fish could see it. But this was like stepping the game up from the junior league to batting at the World Cup, with no training in between.

Still, his companion Steven, though way more experienced, gallantly refused the offer of having a go, and since I was the guide, there was no way in hell this could be my turn, and so Terry was up, no matter what odds were against us. We left Steven on the lookout and went down to cross a safe distance below and started creeping into position.

From our vantage point the entire river ahead was in metallic glare, so bright it was like looking into the sun itself, but we had the fish triangulated against bankside landmarks and Steven was talking us in, not letting us get too close and alerting us with an increasingly shaky voice every time the fish rose, which was often.

These things happen sometimes and we notice and remember them because, though impossible, they did happen and we were there to see it. A trophy trout, a never-ever angler with

The trout did not jump or fight. He simply turned downstream and blurred past us like some underwater meteorite, into the abyss of the pool and the entire tree that was sunken there.

trembling hands, blinding glare. What were the odds? A galactic impossibility.

And, yet, Terry laid out just one cast, miraculously and precisely where it needed to go, and though we could not see a thing we heard Steven cry from his lookout.

'He took it!'

There was no mistaking that: there was a splash as if a brick had hit the water when the line came tight and the fish felt the hook. What happened next probably still haunts Terry's dreams, though realistically it was Nature's way of returning the odds to what they were to begin with.

The trout did not jump or fight. He simply turned downstream and blurred past us like some underwater meteorite, into the abyss of the pool and the entire tree that was sunken there.

The line was still tight, only not to the trophy trout but to the log. We waited long minutes but, for the current strumming on it, it was as if the river was thumbing its nose at us: the line was dead. When we finally agreed to pull it out, it looked as though we may lose the entire fly line. It eventually broke free, coming back with just the stubble of a leader.

Terry was inconsolable. I don't think he truly appreciated the magnitude of what had just happened, the fact that, for once, in all my many years here, I had never even seen a fish of this size much less had a shot at one and hooked it.

'You could have been on a hundred-pound tippet, Terry, and it'd have made no difference,' I said. 'This fish knew exactly what he was doing, and there was no stopping him.'

But Terry kept on about 'losing the fish', the 'bad luck' of being broken off, and hinting just what an amazing photo the fish would have made, a perfect postcard from his first-ever day of fly-fishing. I smiled and nodded with taciturn sympathy, because that's what guides do, and just didn't have the heart to tell him that in reality he never *had* that fish, just touched it, and that in itself would have been a highlight of any angler's life, including my own.

Sadly, after this brightest of fly-fishing debuts, the rest of Terry's week deteriorated into a battle with his own frustrations and inabilities, and I don't recall if he caught another fish, not with me anyway. On the last day, six days into the show, he worked himself up to a frenzy of curses and to the point of throwing in his toys by repeatedly slapping the rising fish with his line or with the sticks he picked up on his backcasts. This was made all the worse by a stark contrast against the attitude and skills of his companion for the day who was not only happy with just being on the river — happy to see the fish rise — but also picking them off with admirably accurate and technical casts. A true angler and a wannabe; you get all sorts in the guiding game. And me, I was again a magician, looking for more white rabbits in my hat, sometimes having to dig deeper than my arm could reach.

It seemed like I got a little too popular and, approached and flattered by a large outfitter, I accepted the role of guiding for them for two months straight, six days a week, rain or shine, which in Southland meant mainly rain or heavy overcast. The people were nice and friendly and brimming with integrity, the money good and the work steady, something any freelancer can appreciate.

Again, there was only one problem. To drum up business, to put 'bums on seats', the outfitter ran frequent promo nights with movies of amazing fly-fishing action in New Zealand. In the said movies, fish were rising everywhere and everyone was catching them, on a dry fly no less. Beer and banter flowed freely, and the idea was that anyone could partake in this trout bonanza, all you had to do was put down your name and the deposit for the trip. You even got a free rod thrown into the deal as a bonus.

The prerequisite skills were mentioned — you had to be able to place a fly on top of a rubbish bin lid from the distance of fifteen metres — though it seems they were not enforced, or perhaps they got diluted with more beer and banter, left out of the contract and context. Until the moments of truth, the first morning on the river with me, when it transpired that out of the entire line-up of willing trout slayers only a couple or three could actually do it, and even then only once in a while.

And bear in mind that casting to a feeding trout — perhaps one of the biggest you've ever seen — is not like taking pot shots at a bin lid with a beer in the other hand. As I often say, when you see the fish, especially a big fish, your casting ability can drop by fifty to eighty per cent and what's left has to be enough to put the fly where it needs to go, ideally within the first couple of attempts.

So, overall, this was like receiving groups of hunters who had never fired a gun before, or at least never hit a target with it, or heli-skiers — all talking steep and deep — but who had actually not yet learnt to ski. It led to some heart-to-heart riverside reality checks. Forgive my directness — I'm told it's a Sagittarian trait so largely the result of my parents' marital scheduling — but, after a number of fish were scared off and flies lost in the vegetation, these conversations would run something like this:

'So, James, you belong to a fly-fishing club, right?'

'Yeah, yeah, mate, been in the club for over twenty years now. We meet every couple of weeks, piss up, tie flies and tell lies, it's all good fun.'

'And, I hear you have casting ponds at the club?'

'Yeah, mate, ponds and platforms, the works. It's a great set-up.'

'And . . . you have instructors too, no?'

'Yeah, we do mate, a few blokes got their triple F certs. Champions, every single one of them.'

'So, James, how come you've never learnt to cast properly?'

Silence.

Still, with perseverance as our only option, and being at it dawn to dusk day after day, we caught fish — plenty of fish — though we spooked many more for every one we caught. And every week the guys had a running scoreboard — who got what, how many, how big and how long — and again the skills were never mentioned, except those of the guides.

There were many nights of merry-making and banter, when the fish grew bigger, the battles more heroic, when all errors were forgotten and fish cleanly smacked with a fly line were called 'refusals'. One thing you had to hand to these people was they had a sense of humour, including an ability to laugh at themselves and their own follies which, considering their performances on the river, was a saving grace, both honest and endearing. So when one night I suggested we needed to change the name of the outfitter to a 'fly-fishing circus' since we already had both the clowns and the magicians, they thought it was an outrageously funny idea, never even considering I didn't mean it as a joke.

I lasted two seasons at the gig, first year with much enthusiasm, the second decidedly less so. I sat through many nights of revelries because 'mingling' was a part of my job, all the while wondering how sharply drawn was the line between clients and friends, how different the selection process, and how the surest way to put you off doing what you loved was to turn it into a job; in the case of fly-fishing, converting its magic and its poetry into a cashflow stream.

Over those two seasons, among the relay of clients new and repeat, there were those who had the time of their lives and who still write to me to this day, asking if or when I am coming back, and others who mainly complained, that the fish were too small, too few or too spooky — the oddest thing considering everyone had pretty much similar experiences.

There was Bazza, stretching out in a lazy-boy recliner beside the fire, sipping a whisky after one of the most epic days we'd had, announcing:

'Ahhh! When I get home from this trip I'll have really big sex with my wife. It's going to be the most intense twenty seconds of my life, and that includes a couple of beers and a smoke afterwards.' And a little retired doctor next to him, frail but perky in his early eighties, giving Bazza some sound medical marital advice: 'I suggest you extend your foreplay by at least thirty seconds.'

There was too, and I'll never forget it, a coming home from a tough day of low spooky rivers and minimal activity to the inevitable:

'How did you go?'

And hearing my client's answer:

'It was crap; we only got seven.'

And thinking to myself: 'Well, you're for sure not fishing with me ever again.'

In the end, the entire experience reminded me why I nearly gave up fly-fishing the first time I started guiding it and just how critically important the process of mutual selection is in this game. A combination of lowest skills and high expectations, and a dismissal of the need for any further learning, is a sure recipe for a riverside comedy of errors, a parody of what fly-fishing is meant to be. It also led me to realise what a peculiar profession a fly-fishing guide was being made to be, especially in New Zealand.

Take mountain guides, for example. I happen to have a number of friends and acquaintances in that community so I get to hear a lot about its ins and outs. It takes and costs an equivalent of a university degree to become a fully qualified mountain guide and, unless you're good at paperwork and business-savvy, you'll probably end up working for a company which has all the necessary concessions. The pay is okay, though certainly not lucrative, considering that you can potentially lose your life, and those of your clients, every time you're out climbing or skiing.

The clients, on the whole, come with a healthy set of expectations. They come for an adventure, to be in the mountains, sure, hopefully to bag a peak or a few if Nature so allows, but you'll never hear the 'no peak no pay' promotions or attitudes. They also sign up for courses and upskill, they train and get fit for their trips, they progress from easier mountains to harder ones.

None of this really applies to guided fly-fishing in New Zealand. Your guide is a freelance with a truck and a bunch of fishing gear, able to roam the entire country, and he's both the student and the sole examiner of his own qualifications. In the course of his work, with even a modicum of common sense, he's unlikely to lose any lives, including his own. The worst that usually happens is that someone falls in and gets wet, and so you go to the nearest pub to warm up, then carry on fishing. His clients too seem to be happy to spend extraordinary amounts of money on their fly-fishing, and this includes the guide, so that his pay is a couple or three times better than that of an equivalent mountain guide.

Nothing wrong with that, I hear you say, sounds like a great job, where do I sign up?

Maybe it is a great job but here's the 'catch'. Again, there are always exceptions, and we pray for those, but more commonly, with all the money poured into a fly-fishing experience come a lot of expectations — not always open but assumed and implied — of catching, a lot and big. The angling media only fuels these: only

the biggest and the best fish make the covers, ads and spreads and if you casually flick through them you can be easily led to believe that this is how the fishing and the fish are in New Zealand, not realising that you're in fact looking at the highlights of the highlights.

Add to this the fact that going after the trout in New Zealand is possibly the hardest, most humbling and technically demanding fly-fishing there is anywhere in the world and you'll see the peculiar challenge the guides face here: how to bridge the gap between what the clients can do and what needs to be done, how to manage their expectations, how to under-promise but over-deliver, and how to, overall, and despite all potential disappointments and frustrations, make every trip as good and as memorable as it can be.

Sometimes this gap between the abilities possessed and required is like a tiny brook and you can leap across it, humming to yourself the praises of how good life happens to be today, other times the gap can be as unbridgeable as the Grand Canyon and looking across it you wonder how we're ever going to get from here to there.

It is another peculiarity of guided anglers that they are prepared to literally burn their money on everything related to the sport — travel, fancy lodges and helicopters, the best gear, attire, books and

Though often — too often — in our instant-gratification world, I see anglers so intent on catching *above all else, they actually forget to fish.*

collectables – except spending it on what matters most, which is their own skills. Remember Flip Pallot, that legendary angler, and his 'last forty feet', the one part that could not be bought but had to be earned?

Years ago I started a fly-fishing academy in the town where I live. It was a no-brainer idea, a sure-bet success. There was so much to learn in fly-fishing that clearly anglers, both new and intermediate, would appreciate someone helping them to disentangle its enigmas. Well, it turned out that, with a few extremely notable exceptions and memorable for their rarity, most people did not want to learn, they just wanted to catch fish. Most expected a brief intro and quick tuition, to be done and over with, to then get on with the business of 'slaying good browns' and 'feisty rainbows'. You can imagine how well that worked out.

The musings on 'the guide and the guided' are nothing new in angling literature, but since I've been on both ends of the stick I thought I'd offer my thoughts on it here for what they are worth. I have been guided by some of the best, and I guided the good and the bad, and a few of the very bad.

In my own guiding, it is not so much the skill level that I'm concerned with but the overall attitude. Any skill can be learnt, if there is enough curiosity, willingness and an open mind. Though often – too often – in our instant-gratification world, I see anglers so intent on *catching* above all else, they actually forget to fish. It is as if the trout was not a fish but some kind of proof and validation of their self-worth. And so, obsessed about the destination, they miss out on the journey, with all its infinite beauty and nuances. As I have said before, there are no short cuts worth taking along this journey, especially not in 'the last forty feet'. Or, as one of my best ever clients put it: 'fly-fishing needs to be like a romantic love affair, not a visit to a whorehouse'.

It is a paradox that, trying to do what we love for a job, we can end up ruining it for ourselves and whoever said 'find out what you love doing, turn that into a job and you'll never work another day in your life' has only looked at one side of the equation. Some guides I know rarely fish for themselves any more. They grow cynical and blasé and act out a 'happy and passionate about it' role only when with clients. As one of them told me: 'If I could get another job I would, but after all the years of guiding I'm pretty much unemployable.' Again, there are inspirational exceptions, but overall I find them not that common. Kids, college fees, house and truck repayments become priorities, daily guiding like shifts in a trout mine.

Recently, ski touring in the Southern Lakes backcountry, I asked a friend mountain guide whether guiding has affected his love for skiing, and if so, how. 'It's always a compromise, and you have to find the middle way, take plenty of time for yourself to restoke your fire so that the whole thing does not become just a job,' he said. 'The money is not great, but you get to ski powder every time you work, and you always get to go first.'

Oh yes, the elusive Middle Way, as in guiding so in life. In guided fly-fishing we rarely get to 'go first' though with the right people, and during a good hatch I had never as yet turned down the clients' invitation to join in. Some even insisted on it. 'We learn as much if not more from watching you fish than from you explaining to us how to do it; it's a lot better to see it in action,' they'd say.

So, forever mindful of treading the Middle Way, even if at times for a spell losing it completely, I'm not giving up guiding anytime soon. I just get more and more selective who I want to be on a river with, whether there is money involved or not. This is not to judge anglers as people, just to recognise that we are all different, and free to be so, and also seeing that, in the 'guide and the guided' interaction roughly three states are possible — harmony, wait-till-it's-all-over numbness, or straight-out disharmony — and to me, for one, rivers and trout are too precious and sacred to bring the latter two scenarios to them, or to create them there.

The ideas of 'to guide or not to guide' and — something I rarely considered myself before — 'to be guided or not' revealed to me a whole new level of insight and depth since I've been fishing and spending much river and mountain time with Jennifer's father. Brit has fished for over sixty-five years now. He has been everywhere of note, caught whatever fish were to be found there, and, along the way, he probably spent more money on guides and fly-fishing travel than many people spend on their mortgages.

Brit fishes most days, unless he ties flies, or skis, so it was only natural that, when I arrived into a Colorado spring and a trout world that was completely new to me but intimately familiar to him, we instantly fell into a kind of fly-fishing "bromance" of the finest kind.

'Derek and I will be doing a lot of fishing together, most days probably,' Brit announced, 'and you Jennifer, you're of course welcome to join us whenever you're free.'

And she rolled her eyes and said: 'Da-ad! He's my boyfriend, not yours!'

Over the two months that followed we spent many 'best days ever' together, fishing the early-season hatches on the Fryingpan and the Roaring Fork, Speying the Colorado, or drift-fishing with Brit's regular river companion Tim Heng, a retired guide and a fly shop manager. Brit showed me the finer points of Spey and I managed to return him to single-hand casting, reasoning that, despite his injured shoulder, laying out fifty to sixty feet of a 3-wt line did not require almost any shoulder action at all.

Just as thrilling were the tailgate après-fishing conversations, buzzing with energy and intensity like some high-voltage power information exchange. It became clear during those free-flow dialogues that Brit did not really like to be guided, though he certainly appreciated the guides' expertise.

'I've fished for trout and other river and lakes species most of my life, but when I first began fly-fishing for bones and tarpon on saltwater flats, and Spey-casting for steelhead in Canada, I was completely dependent on instruction from the guides,' he told me. 'But, as soon as I started catching fish I realised that the guide's presence diminished my sense of personal accomplishment.

'When I caught a fish following a guide's instructions and corrections, I felt the guide deserved credit for the fish, and I was just being a good student,' he went on. 'So, as soon as I felt able and as often as I can, I get the guides to take me to the water and ask them to leave me there, though I may ask their assistance with

'You see, at this stage of my life, how a fish is caught has become more important to me than the fact that it is caught at all,' he said.

any problems I can't resolve on my own.'

Having seen him fish, I thought there wouldn't be too many of those situations, and it would be probably the guides who would benefit to stick around and watch him in action, just as I have.

'I've never met a saltwater guide who can't spot fish quicker than I can, or a steelhead guide who isn't a far better Spey-caster than me,' Brit said. 'And when I fish alone, there's no doubt I catch fewer fish than if the guide was by my side, but I feel that every fish was caught by me. I am also free to innovate and experiment if I want, sometimes with approaches contrary to what the guide has insisted on. This freedom to experiment adds an element of excitement and anticipation. When my experiments fail to produce, I learn something. But when they succeed, the satisfaction is heightened.'

Then, as he did religiously on all our fishing or skiing outings, Brit produced his hip flasks neatly labelled with his copperplate handwriting, Laphroaig and Jameson.

'You see, at this stage of my life, how a fish is caught has become more important to me than the fact that if it is caught at all,' he said.

And we drank to that, because these were my sentiments, too, exactly to a word.

chapter 11

THE LITTLE CREEK MEANDERING through the tussocks was one of Brendan's favourites, but as we were getting ready to fish it I saw that he was not rigging up.

'Aren't you taking your rod?' I asked.

'No, there aren't that many fish here and I know where they all are. Let's just take your rod and see how it goes. I can always borrow it.'

We walked down and away from the water for maybe three-quarters of an hour, found the creek again and started to look. It was narrower than a single lane, mostly about half of it, and it had long stony riffles, shallow and fast, but it also cut deep sharp canyon-like corners overhung with matagouri, flax and toetoe and these would make perfect habitat for reclusive brown trout. The water was dark — too dark to see into — which made the creek a dry-fly only proposition. Brendan assured me that, even if there were absolutely no hatches elsewhere, you could usually find rising fish here, never many but enough, providing there was no wind and today seemed just about perfect.

Not that the fish would be giveaways! The feed lines in the creek were well-defined but tight against the high bank and the first trout we found was tucked right into the corner of the pool, protected from above by a man-sized matagouri, bristled with thorns.

I nodded in quiet appreciation.

'Now, this trout knows where to be, huh!' There were barely inches in front of the fish where you could place the fly, not to mention the dreaded barbed-wire bush above, and yet the fish was rising so happily there was a slow but perceptible beat to his feeding.

Brendan smiled as we watched the spectacle.

'I don't bring anyone here because it's like this — too tight and too hard — and most people wouldn't get it so why even bother trying,' he said. 'But these are magnificent fish and every one is worth catching. If you're up for a challenge.'

I was, though even with a tight side-cast I managed to hang up on the thorny bush on the first try, and the second, and the third. Each time I slowly pulled the line back, mindful that any sharp movement could wrap the tippet around a branch or, worse, shake it right above the fish. On another cast I hang up again, but this time right in the corner and ahead of the fish. As I slowly withdrew the line, the fly pulled free and dropped into the water with all the gentleness of a natural mayfly.

The fish rose, but I felt Brendan's hand steadying my shoulder.

'No! It's not you,' he said.

The fish rose again.

'Now!'

I lifted, felt solid weight and a big splash, then twang! The trout had broken off.

'Bugger! That was so good!' Brendan was a definition of calm. 'Maybe your tippet weakened through all the pulling through the thorns.'

A couple of pools up we found another fish, also tight against the high bank, though this time with no overhead obstacles.

'You have a go,' I said, passing my rod to Brendan. But he wouldn't have it.

'No, you go. I can come back here anytime. I want to see you catch a fish first. I get as much pleasure out of it, if not more.'

I cast, clean and easy, with a good lead on the fish, but in the metallic glare on the water I immediately lost the sight of my fly. The fish rose and I lifted the rod. There was a sound like a plucking kiss and I saw that my fly was still a good two feet ahead of the trout and I just pulled it out of the water.

'Shit! I've spooked him!' I heard myself say. Why was my voice, my whole body, trembling so much?

But the fish rose again, clearly undisturbed, and I cast, and this time there were no mistakes, no mishaps.

'Don't let him go anywhere,' Brendan cautioned. 'Lots of pressure!'

Following the fish down the creek would not be an option here, an impossible obstacle course of high banks and thorny bushes, and so I kept the fish in the pool, at times kneeling down to get a stronger angle on the rod. He tired quickly and Brendan netted him for me.

The trout was close to five pounds, but it was not his size — though remarkable for such a small creek — that was his most striking feature. It was the colour. The belly was dark orange, like the darkest whisky or the spawning plumage of a brook trout, and it further darkened towards his back but for fiery-red speckles on his flanks. Except for his unmistakable predatory shape the fish looked like no brown trout I've ever seen, though he was camouflaged perfectly against the dark tannin-rich water of the creek and the golden-black rocks that studded its bottom.

Brendan was happy and the shakes in my body were slowly dissipating.

The fish rose and I lifted the rod. There was a sound like a plucking kiss and I saw that my fly was still a good two feet ahead of the trout and I just pulled it out of the water.

'This creek has been really good to me,' he said. 'It was as good a fish as I'd ever seen out of here, size and colour.'

'Okay, your turn now,' I said. 'I want to see you catch one too.'

But for the rest of the walk we did not see another trout.

Remembering this entire episode – which took place some seasons ago, though it is still as vivid in my memory as if it happened this morning – made me think not so much of the fish I've caught over the years but of the people I caught them with, those who helped or made it all possible, or who had just been there, companions in adventure.

Sure, being something of a 'lone wolf' by nature and choice, I have done a lot – A LOT – of fishing on my own and with my dogs. Fishing on your own is a good test of character and its depth because, frankly, if you cannot be a good companion to yourself alone how can you be that to others? Fishing with dogs is perhaps the easiest of all: they are always happy, never argue or talk back, never question your decision. You don't need to take turns either, so you get all the opportunities.

Some of my most memorable outings happened this way, those 'once in the lifetime' days when everything aligns just right, when the trout activity is so off the charts it totally consumes you with a mixture of feverish greed, uncontainable joy and the sheer rod-tip-to-the-knuckle physicality that leaves you both drained and fulfilled, and trembling with TTs (trutta tremens), and thinking at the end of it all that if this would happen to be last day of your life, this would be a fine and high note to finish on.

One such day was given to me and Maya on the West Coast during a cicada season. The bush was deafening with the song of cicadas and the trout were so keyed in on the sound of big bugs falling into the water you could have thrown in a twig and they'd have come to investigate it. I would have caught over 100 lbs of brown trout that day and if there were any smaller fish in that river I didn't catch any. No, these brutes were coming in at six to eight pounds, their mouths already wide open while still a distance away from my Clark's Cicadas. I was battling one and I could already see another trout ten to twenty metres above, and I knew he would take too, and on the first cast.

Then there were the hatches on the lower Mataura where I chanced upon a pod of apparently fresh fish — they seemed totally unaware of what the fly-fishing game meant for them, and they were certainly larger than the average residents — and in a 300-metre-long pool I left no trout uncaught, and all on my 3 wt and #16 dries.

There were also similar days in the Central North Island where along a foot-wide feed line tight against the papa cliffs there would be large trout rising nose to tail, a dozen or more in each pool, and the only reason I could not pick them all off was because a fighting fish would spook its closest neighbours, though nowhere near as much or as many as I would expect on the rivers I usually fish in the South Island. And hauling in those 5-lb rainbows, with fiercely hooked kypes and horsepower to match, I kept looking around, thinking, 'Surely people must know about this, surely someone would show up any moment now and want to partake of this dry-fly insanity.' But, at least on the days I was there, no one ever did.

This, you understand, is not bragging, just some of the brightest highlights of my thirty years on New Zealand trout rivers. If you're out there that long, you're bound to get extra lucky here and there. Yet even then, amid the adrenal high and overflowing gratitude, there was a sense that something important — perhaps a lot more than the fish — was missing from the experience. Jennifer experienced this too and she put it into words during one of our riverside campfire evenings.

'For years I fished alone and I've been totally happy in my trout world, but there was always this feeling shadowing all those experiences, a sense that this was too much fun and joy not to share it with someone, someone close, someone who really gets it at, at least, a similar level to my own.'

Ideally, someone who is there for the same reasons and similar philosophy, who can derive as much pleasure or even more by helping the other to catch a fish and who can laugh equally when either of you goofs up. A friend, real and true, with whom to camp, and eat, and drink by the river, who can be an honest shrink when you need one, and who can create and relive the trout moments with you, and mirror them back to you magnified manifold.

Maybe we only come to that later in our fly-fishing evolution, when the initial hunger and the greed of the intermediate have been satiated, when we've caught enough fish so there is nothing to prove and brag about, when the whole thing becomes a lot more of an inner game than what I term an 'exercise in accounting' and the gathering of meaningless social-media accolades.

If I appear to ramble here it is because the most obvious often most easily escapes us and so, as Henry David Thoreau told us already, 'Many men go fishing all of their lives without knowing that it is not fish they are after,' and I for one had long ago swore to never again make that mistake. So I propose to you an idea that our best catches ever are the friends we make on the excuse of chasing cold-blooded creatures together. With time, trout tallies fade into insignificance, but the memories of such friendships are like precious stones polished by river water.

The point is, gender or age differences aside, fly-fishing is like sex: it matters absolutely who you're doing it with. Which begets an interesting question: how does the guiding fit into it and where?

When you mix love and money things can get complicated and often at the expense of purity. While guiding you play a role — depending on the skill level of your charges, something between a companion, a facilitator and a magician, or any combination thereof. When it's really good it feels like no work at all, when it's bad you'd think you're doing a stint in a gulag or worse.

I've been both places so I know by direct experience: some of my most precious human encounters came by the way of guiding — I may have already mentioned Jennifer. And a few of the most horrid, soul-numbing days, too, when the river was boiling with rising trout, and yet we blanked, and it was on me because I apparently didn't know the right fly, and no one would mention the awkward truth that fish would rarely take any fly within the rod-length from an angler, which is about as far as the punters could cast.

So I've experienced both extremes and along the way I've learnt to discern. Now, I turn down more work than I take on. Like the very trout we hunt, I've become selective. So when an enquiry comes that reads something like:

'There are six of us and none of us has fly-fished before. We'd like to go somewhere remote and catch a few nice fish, but we only have half a day. What can you recommend?'

I suggest a salmon farm and fortunately never hear back from the good people.

Compare this to the same-week correspondence from Trevor, an Aussie bloke who — despite his ailing health — always radiates enthusiasm and good cheer:

'Robert and I are coming Thursday night. Can't wait to fish with you again. Last time was so good! Don't forget your guitar, evenings are long this time of year. And BTW, I'll be doing all the cooking. Robert is a banker and all he can cook is books.'

Do you see the difference? It's like trout, having to choose between a cigarette butt and a mouse.

Still, I'm happy to report that those horrid days — the 'what am I doing here?' and 'never again' interminable hours of fly-fishing as travesty of its pure and noble self — are relatively rare and the more acute my discernment the more infrequent they become. Otto, both client and a friend who woke me up several times during one of our trips *coming back* from his pre-dawn casting practice, and who otherwise had the time of his life fishing in New Zealand, told me about a Florida tarpon guide who had taken the art of discernment to the level of utmost purity.

He would show up in the morning to pick up his prospective clients for the day, and after the initial pleasantries in the parking lot, he would pull out a fully rigged-up rod and ask them: 'Here, show me your cast.' When you know what to look for, you can see within the first few moments and movements whether someone has got it or not. If they did, the guide would take them fishing. If they didn't, he'd politely say something like 'Hey, that's really great, but let's not waste each other's time. Casting like that, the tarpon just ain't gonna happen.'

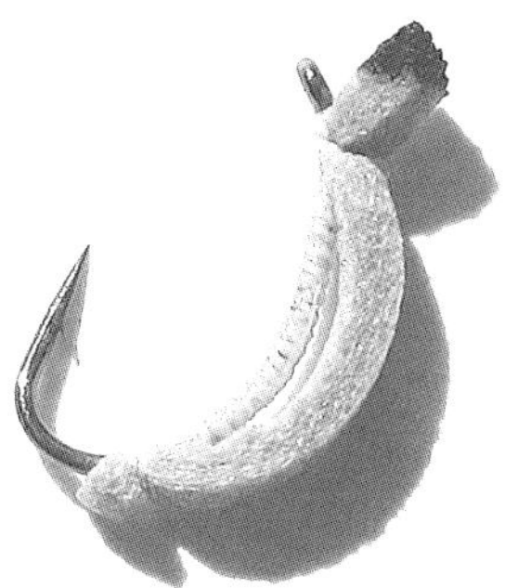

Man after my own heart, I thought. Clearly, I still had ways to go to get to that level, but here was something to aspire to. Yes, it was possible to mix love for fly-fishing with money, but discernment and selectivity were critical to protect both the art and yourself. Otherwise, you could end up lampooning around your beloved waters, going through the motions and smiles, counting money in your mind, while your soul wept and howled.

Some of the most influential, important and dear people in my life have come into it through fly-fishing and the pursuit of trout and the places where these remarkable creatures live. I won't bore you with the list of names and events; if you've fished long enough I'm sure you've got your own. And if you haven't, you're in for a treat because you're yet to encounter them. Suffice to say, without those river friends, my life, such as it is, would be inconceivably poorer, the fishing itself not nearly as fulfilling, so, though I get ever more discerning and selective, I'm also always on a lookout for like-minded trout hunters, potential river friends I have not yet met. This meeting of river minds and souls elevates our pursuit to a level far above the sum of its mechanical or even aesthetic parts.

To me, in this dumbed-down age of instant gratifications, least resistance and effort, a fly angler on a river is a sign of hope. Fly-fishing is a complex art and so it tends to attract interesting people. As fly anglers, we take a higher challenge knowing that the rewards will be greater and more meaningful because of it, and these days this is a rare attitude, certainly worth noticing and encouraging.

Looking back at some of my own river friendships, I only wish I had been more aware of just how precious those moments were, at the time, while they were happening. Not taking them for granted, or as normal or ordinary, realising that they won't be around forever. Why? Because some of those people are now gone. There won't ever be any more wine-fuelled discussions and dinners at Madame Colette's table and even as I write this somewhere in a small town in western France, Grandpa Trout — nearly ninety now — is in his last days and breaths, his voice feeble, his spirit already partly gone (he passed away as this book was going into print). I still so vividly remember him catching his best-ever trout on the River X, one I had taken him to, when for once he did not lecture me on the advantages of fishing blind over spotting the trout first. His tirades annoyed me at times, now I cannot tell you how much I wish I could hear them again or what would I give to revisit those times. But they are a part of a bygone era and that in itself has been a priceless lesson.

And so I've learnt, and am still learning, about the priorities, about what really matters most, and about the art of appreciating events and people in real time — what's happening while it's happening and who with — not later, when it all becomes a nostalgic memory. What is the most obvious eludes us most easily and no reminders are too frequent.

I was back with Brendan, on our annual and almost ritualistic early-season outing in Southland. One day we fished another small creek, this one full of large trout which were yet to drop down into the main river, and it seemed to me we were doing a really poor job of it. In a full day of intense effort — spotting fish for each other and climbing up and down the banks, bush-bashing through the willow and gorse and tiptoeing against the deep current to the limits of our chest waders — we saw and fished to over twenty trout, but hooked only one each and promptly lost them both.

I was more than just a little agitated with frustration.

'Man, what are we doing wrong? There's fish everywhere and we can't catch any,' I said in the camp that night. 'It should have been an amazing day, like last year, and yet we've barely connected with the trout.'

We were in our camping chairs on the riverbank and Brendan poured out his favourite Laphroaig and looked at me long and hard to make sure I was paying attention.

'If you spent just an hour with me at work you'd realise how fortunate we are just to be here, doing what we do,' he said.

In his other life, Brendan is a top nurse at the regional hospital's palliative care unit or, as he calls it, 'the end of the road ward'.

'It was still an amazing day, catching fish or not,' he went on. Of course, deep down I knew that, but how easily we forget, how easily we lose perspective.

The next day, we were on another stunning piece of water and there were trout in it too. We spotted one on a lip of a corner pool and Brendan, as he does so often, was already moving out of the way of a cast, and suggesting what fly I should put on, until I interrupted him.

'No, no, no, my friend, this time, it is definitely your turn,' I said.

And this time too there were no mishaps, no mistakes. I was there, right beside him through all of it, until the fish, released and free, nosed into the lee of the current created by our boots, and we watched it silently for a long time, and it all felt as good — better — than if I caught it myself.

It never fails to surprise me that, come about this time of year, the majority of anglers — okay, except for diehards of Taupo and Rotorua — put away their gear and begin the long and wistful wait for the new season that is still months away. There is some merit to that since such interlude away from trout waters makes the heart for them grow fonder, and we've all experienced that thinking about going fishing — the planning, anticipating, tying flies and readying gear — are just as enjoyable and integral a part of our pursuit as the trout hunting itself.

The point I'm making is this, though, in New Zealand you never need to hang up your fishing gear to enter into this enforced piscatorial hibernation. Even with minimal bit of research you can always find a place to fish, any day of the year. Which is why I for one have never suffered from either the withdrawal symptoms or the 'opening day' fever, because, well, my trout season never really ends.

There is a seasonal circularity to the year of trout, as elegant as it is varied, a calendar of fishing 'events' which are a delight to follow, and being on the water only during the traditional October-to-April season you are missing a good part of them. If you have fished long enough you probably know about the end-of-winter stillwater and the early-season nymphing, the spring's first mayflies, the arrival of green and brown beetles, the snowstorm-like nights of caddis hatches when you seem to need goggles every time you turn on your head-torch, the summertime of bumbling cicadas and backcountry blowflies, the willow-grub days and the autumn spinner falls.

But have you ever come across a pod of winter fish so large and dense it made the bottom of the river shimmer black and you had a chance to put your fly through the middle of it? Or walked up a small tributary stream seeing dozens upon dozens of paired-up brown trout, and felt beaten up and dejected by their total disinterest in your flies? Until you came across a trophy rainbow in their midst, and he took on the first cast, and pulled you upstream several hundred metres scattering untold number of other trout, and you got to touch his ferocious-looking kype as you unhooked him, and you knew he'd forever remain one of the most memorable fish of your life.

The key skill in fishing through what I've come to call 'the other half of the season' is observation and the flexibility to change and adapt your approach, gear and techniques to the ways of trout, and to what they are doing at the time. This was made obvious to me one autumn day on a well-known river at the Southern Lakes. It was mid-May or so, though running on the season's momentum we were still intensely in a sight-fishing mode. Sure enough, we saw a lot of fish, but they were all browns, in pairs and pods and not much interested in feeding. We managed a hook-up here and there, with a nymph and an odd dry, but overall it was a tough and dispiriting string of endless refusals. Then, on the way back, we met an elderly chap who was fishing up behind us. He had already landed a couple of nice fish and was upbeat about a few more.

'What did you get them on?' we asked.

'Streamers, of course,' he said, 'they won't take anything else.'

True that. Lesson learnt.

As the temperatures drop and the days grow short, sight-fishing is no longer a viable option. The sun is low, shadows deep and the glare can be intense. Besides, with not much insect life around, the fish are deep on the bottom so you're unlikely to see them anyway. Unless the day warms up enough for a hatch or spinner fall. For example, the Mataura below Gore is now open until the end of May and the dry fly can be sensational right up to the final curtain.

Sure, you need to pick your days — sunny and still — but even a taste of late-autumn Mataura magic, when the light is like liquid gold and trout slurp dries all around you, will make you want to come back again and again, to make it your own 'trout event', even if you have to sit out the firsts of winter storms.

June is the toughest month, truly the bottom of the cycle, and it feels like it too, but make it through the winter solstice and things are on the up again. In and above water there is a sense of new beginning.

To really make the most of fishing through 'the other half of the season' it helps if you have access to rainbow trout waters, especially large lake systems. Rainbows spawn much later than browns, and they spend much of late autumn and winter feeding aggressively, often on brown trout eggs and juveniles. Silicone smelt flies (like those for imitating whitebait) can be especially effective, and the takes are among the most violent and decisive you ever get to experience when fly-fishing for trout, totally different from say a take on an egg or booby which can feel slow and dull, more like a snag.

My standard kit for winter fishing involves a shooting-head line, which is a distinctly Taupo set-up yet extremely rare to see outside that region. I've used it for years at the Southern Lakes and only occasionally met an angler who seemed to know what I was doing. A shooting head is a short (ten metres or so) sink-like-a-brick line attached to braided and, more recently, floating backing which acts as the running line. To fish with it properly you need a stripping basket to retrieve the coils into and to organise them neatly for the next cast.

Shooting heads (SH) work particularly well with floating flies, like those which have foam built into them, boobies for example, or deliberately buoyant streamers. Usually, you'd tie streamers to make them heavy so they sink well, but with a shooting head this weight is unnecessary as the line does all the sinking. So the line drags along the bottom and the fly floats up above it, and you can tweak just how high by the length of your tippet and perhaps the speed of retrieve as well.

With the SH lines it is easy to cast long distances, twenty-five metres plus, providing you load the rod well, and shoot the line, and the backing does not foul. All you need to do is to find the 'sweet' amount of overhead — the length of backing past the rod tip — which works best for your set-up. Any more than five feet is likely to be too much, and the heavy line will start dropping, the cast collapsing. With even a modicum of practice, a shooting-head line will become your preferred choice for any streamer fishing. It casts far and effortlessly, with short backcast and no need for false casting. It also gives maximum 'bottom time' to your fly. When, as in winter, fish are mainly on the bottom, you want to get there quickly and stay there as long as possible.

Double-handed Spey casting — as you have read already — has become another of my winter favourites, ideal for streamer fishing and for big rivers, places like the Clutha, lower Waitaki or the Tongariro, and the lower reaches and mouths of other big rivers, most of which are open all year. Since the arrival of LOOP in New Zealand, we now have access to full range of Spey gear and the style will only get more popular.

The easiest way to get into Spey is through its Scandi style which uses, again, the shooting heads attached to running lines. The Scandi lines can be floating or sinking but both go like a shot and with a 13 to 16-foot rod you'll surprise yourself just how far you can cast and how much water you cover. Good Spey casting takes a lot of practice, both on the grass and on the water, so learning and putting it to good use makes for a perfect winter project. Just don't try to figure it out by yourself as it's a recipe for frustration, maybe even giving up. Get lessons or DVD tutorials, ideally both. Like any true art, Spey seems extremely complex when you first get into it, but with time, practice and guidance, it reveals itself to you, poetry of motion, and like me, you may get hooked on the sheer aesthetics of the cast, and the finesse it brings out in you.

By August, the rainbow fishing is nearing its peak and on the water it does not feel like winter any more. Not unlike spawning salmon, the rainbows come in waves so timing and the element of luck play their part. I usually fish for an hour or two every few days and so get both the lows and the highs of the runs. This is a pleasantly relaxing and social way of fishing too, where another angler is welcome company and not an intruder on 'your' river or beat. The fish come and go so spooking them is not an issue; they are the dwellers of the deep and thus innocent of danger we present to them, certainly not like the wary late-season browns suspiciously looking over their 'shoulders' at the slightest disturbance.

In August too, and often earlier depending on winter, the whitebait begin to migrate from the sea and into the rivers and trout — often large trout — both sea-run and resident follow the runs and gorge themselves on the little translucent squirts. The mouths of rivers, especially on the West Coast, are prime locations for this kind of fishing, though you may want to indulge it before the whitebaiting season opens as the 'baiters, intent on their own game, tend to get grumpy if someone with a fly rod gets in front of them and scares off their little fish. Fly-fishing for whitebaiting sea-run trout is a real hit-and-miss game, and it has certainly been more of a miss for me, but the Coast in winter is glorious beyond words. The weather is stable and settled for days, there is snow on the hills, beach campfires, sunsets in the sea and no sandflies, so hunting big sea-runs is a kind of lottery in which you can't really lose.

Then, as the days grow longer and the light improves, you start noticing the early browns coming back into the lake margins, skinny and spent, and not always worth fishing for but a joy to see, like swallows announcing the arrival of spring. They feed voraciously, quickly regaining their lost form, and by mid-September, sometimes earlier, the stillwater fishing at the lakes is at its prime.

The best cure for winter blues and the 'opening day' fever alike is the season without end so give your rod and waders an airing or two this winter, become a part of the trout world through the quiet months as well. They may be quiet for us, but for trout they are a time of intense activity. You will learn a lot about their ways, see huge pods of fish going up to spawn, witness trout chasing bullies at speeds that blur the eye, maybe even get to touch their bodies so glacially cold, you'll feel they may give you frostbite. And then, before you know it, it's October again.

Only that, for me, this October would be like no other — Jennifer was coming back to New Zealand, this time not to see 'how things go' but to stay with me for part of the season, to fish and live the trout nomad lifestyle which she was so enchanted with and converted to as if it was the most natural choice ever. It seemed that if my *Trout Bohemia* was a heartfelt enquiry into the nature of fly-fishing relationships, and perhaps a subconscious call to the Universe if there was one out there for me as well, this was at once an answer, a test and an opportunity to live what I'd learnt.

Sure, many adjustments would be needed because, if you haven't gathered already, fishing with a girl is well . . . very, very different.

chapter 12

LIPSTICKS, NAIL FILES, EYELINERS. A yoga necklace and matching earrings. Hairbrush, combs and hair ties and of course mirrors, one double-sided with a magnifier, and a spare one too, though the phone's camera might work as well, but only in emergencies. Hat for the fishing, and another one for getting there, both with matching buffs, and a shirt colour-coordinated with socks. A safari mini skirt, with inbuilt shorts, in case it's windy. Watch out trout! This girl is going fishing!

Then a moment of doubt . . .

'Oh crap!' she says. 'I forgot my Gink. Have you got any I can borrow?'

'Of course. I've brought a spare one for you.'

'You mean it? Really? Oh, you're wonderful! And you've got my rod, right?'

'Your rod, and your reel, your waders and boots, and everything else too.'

'Fabulous, darling. Have you seen my fly box?'

'No, but I've got enough flies for both of us.'

You are both on the way to the river and she is beside herself with excitement, like a child going to a playground, chattering nonstop, about other times you fished together, and how great it was, every time, the fish that got away and those that didn't, the flowers and the bugs she saw, the birds and the moon, and other things you never noticed, and you dare not interrupt because it all sounds like happy music.

On the bank, you are ready in no time because the fish are rising and she just smiles and says:

'You go and start fishing. I'll be right with you.'

A long while later, you're landing your second fish, and see another that will eat just as eagerly, and so you turn to look at the truck, and there she is, smiling and waving and yelling something like 'I'm almost ready, just putting on a new leader.'

'You need help?'

'No, I'm fine. Done it a million times.'

And oddly, you don't mind the delays, the chatter and the tangles. Instead, you listen and your heart glows with fondness and anticipation because you know that, no matter what — the trout and insect activity, the weather or river conditions — it's going to be a good day. Or, as she would put it, 'the best day ever!'.

If you have never fished with a woman angler, let me tell you upfront there is much we blokes can learn from spending time on the water with the girls, both in approach and attitude, but above all in pure simplicity and the softness of touch they bring to the sport. I first became aware of it years ago while reading a couple of anthologies of women writing about fishing, *A Different Angle: Fly Fishing Stories by Women*, and *Uncommon Waters: Women Write About Fishing*, both edited by Holly Morris. Since then, I've been fortunate to fish with a number of female anglers, all as skilled as they are passionate, and it's become even more evident to me that women not only fish differently but for different reasons too.

When I first met Jennifer, who has since become my partner and my best fishing buddy, she told me she didn't care if she caught fish. And I thought to myself: yeah right, how many times I've heard that one before, usually from fishing clients, trying to pre-empt any shortfalls of their skills once we actually found a feeding trout. And so it took me days, weeks even, to realise that she not only meant it but lived it too. It's not like she went to the river just to look at the trout; she's fished with passion, and intensity, and skill, but there was no pressure and no expectations, just the simple joy of being there doing it. Oddest thing was that I had arrived at this attitude too, but it had taken me thousands of fish and many years of 100-plus days on the water. She was there from day one — with nothing to prove but with an open mind and a sense of wonder that a fish, big or small, would actually come and look, and possibly even take the clump of feathers she threw in front of it, and how every time it was a gift and a miracle.

So many anglers these days go to the river with scales, tape measure and the mission to prove themselves — and the 4G Wi-Fi to instantly let the world know about their greatness and achievements — it seems to me we have lost the perspective of what fly-fishing was meant to be: a mystical return to Nature and quietude, not an ego-boosting exercise in accounting and conquest. But so often today a fish is likely to be on Facebook before it's back in the water, and this has become the new normal, though one I've never cared about. Which is why — and please forgive me fellas — after nearly thirty years of fly-fishing, and much time guiding, I've come to favour fishing with a girl, and maybe a little bit like her too, and it feels like a breath of fresh air and a return to purity and the true values of the sport.

'There is more BS in fly-fishing than in a Texas cattle yard,' the late Lefty Kreh is famous for saying and you know what he meant: the self-professed experts and *addicts* who not only think they know

'There is more BS in fly-fishing than in a Texas cattle yard,' the late Lefty Kreh is famous for saying . . .

everything but insist on telling you all about it, and force upon you ALL their iPhone grip-n-grins, whether you want it or not. (I have developed a healthy and sanity-preserving guideline for myself here: the more people talk at you about fishing, usually the less they know; the ones I really want to learn from charge money for the info.) Again, refreshingly – and with some famous exceptions, though don't ask me to mention any names here – you won't find women anglers doing that. They are more likely to be asking questions, and good ones too, like 'Can the trout actually warn each other of the danger posed by an approaching angler?' and if you have fished long enough you'll know this is a valid question even if the answer seems to defy our current understanding.

Fly selection, as practised by a fly-fishing girl, certainly does that too. You'll rarely find her upturning rocks, seining the current or throwing about big Latin words like *Pteronarcys* or *Oniscigaster*. 'I just open the fly box and pick a fly that *speaks* to me most,' Jen told me. 'Usually it's the colour. Pretty flies are a lot more fun to fish with than the drab ones.'

One day in Colorado, we drove up to fish the Grand Mesa, a high-alpine plateau pocked with some 200 lakes, all full of trout. Looking from the car at the first lake we came to we saw there were fish rising everywhere and so we rigged up and started catching them pretty much from the first cast on. They were all stocked rainbows, weak and never more than a pound, but they were taking dries like they had never seen a fly before, and we fished barbless as we always do, and so it was all a good sport. Jen is a *screamer* – when she hooks up and especially when she loses a fish, often both, and soon the lake had its own echoing soundscape of frequent cries, laughter and an odd profanity. I had never been here before or examined the local bug life, so I had on a most generic 'looks like everything' fly I could think of, in between a mayfly and a caddis, and the fish were not refusing it, which made me think I had somehow instinctively 'matched the hatch'. Jen too was catching one fish after another, and although I could not always see her through the ponderosa pines which came right down to the water, I heard all the action. After a while it all got a bit silly — we would have caught some fifty fish between us — and so I stopped and walked over to her.

'What are you using, love?' I asked.

'This,' she said, showing me a big yellow foam beetle. 'I liked the colour, it's happy and goes well with my hat. Fish seem to like it too.'

There was no arguing with that.

'The difference in the ways women approach fly-fishing is especially clear when you teach them, something we do a lot of,' Kristina Royter, one of the most vocal and active advocates for the *sisterhood of the angle* in Australasia, told me. 'Guys would be like "Yep . . . yep . . . I already know that," — even if they don't, really — "Yep . . . yep . . . got any tips for catching the big ones?" Women, on the other hand, would listen and learn every step of the way. We don't overthink stuff or force anything. We take our time — why rush a good thing? — and we bring certain tenderness and finesse to our fly-fishing. It's more a contemplation for us and not a race or proving grounds. We certainly don't go out to "rip lips" but more to flirt with the trout.'

And on the subject of flirting a trout girl: on the uppermost Clutha above where I live there are a few decent-size brown trout which I see almost daily during my dog walks. There are no pools here, only bankside pockets and current lines breaking off gravel protuberances, and from above the fish are predictable to locate and easy to see, especially as they glint in the sun when sipping *Deleatidium* spent spinners that this part of the river is renowned for.

I have caught some of them in the past, but only in the earliest days of a season or at the change of light because, encountering anglers almost daily, these fish are nigh impossible to fool, the badass customers who have seen it all, and who don't even spook, just merely stop feeding to let you pass.

The most prominent of those fish, who is always there, in the feed line a few metres above a large broom bush, we nicknamed Bruce and, during one of our dog walks I said to Jennifer, 'If you catch Bruce, I'll propose to you.' She laughed and this had become our household joke, with Bruce the uncatchable being about as safe a bet as you could ever make.

The other day Jen went out fishing for a couple of hours and came back in tears.

'I had him! I hooked him! I hooked Bruce!' she sobbed.

'You did? What happened?'

'He went out into the main current, jumped and . . . the fly came out.'

I thought, 'Bruce, mate! Phew! That was close!'

But to Jennifer I said: 'Well done, love! You've hooked him and he was the impossible fish. Counts as caught to me. Tell you what, though. There's another river I want to show you and tomorrow looks like a good day for it, and we can nominate any fish as Bruce so I can be there while you catch it. We'll have a fabulous day.'

A smile came through her tears, like a sun reappearing from behind clouds.

'Really? You mean it? Like, the best day ever?'

And I thought: fishing with you, every day is the best ever. And then I told her that because girls like to hear such things.

Beyond the silly stereotypes of *Women in Waders* calendars that adorn many a fly-tying den, and beyond other staged photos of chicks with fish and rods flooding your social media channels, women in angling are a genuine and steadily growing force. Jennifer has just helped run a Ladies on the Fly event in Colorado which proved a sold-out success, and Kristina Royter tells me there are a lot more genuinely passionate female anglers out there than meets the eye. If you ever get a chance to fish with one of them — not someone you've dragged to the river to show off your prowess with the rod but one who loves fishing of her own free will — seize the opportunity with all you can. It can do a lot of good to your fishing; it's done wonders for mine.

'I'm trying to hurry! Going as fast as I can,' Jennifer said, putting on her mascara. It just wouldn't do going fly-fishing for trout looking like a frump.

You might have guessed, we were going to the river again. But like a river, unstoppable and wild, time had flowed and much has changed. By now, I was spending so much time in Colorado that the immigration officials began asking where was it that I actually lived permanently, and New Zealand had become Jennifer's new spiritual trout home, her happiest place.

Gone was her punk-rock casting and the carelessness of approach, and any goof-ups were now like jokes well told and acted out, not reasons for frustration or upsets. Over a couple of years we shook things down, including how to be together — not all roses and kisses when you get two obsessively independent individuals with strong views on a range of subjects — and how to allow for each other's freedoms and idiosyncrasies. And so finally we could fish like equals, hiking the rivers hand in hand, taking turns, spotting trout for each other, and just being there together. The presence of the other, both in heart-stopping moments of excitement and in companionable silences alike, magnified all the trout experiences we had, elevating them to a level far above anything either of us could reach doing it solo.

Jennifer began to host some of my fishing trips and she was an instant win with the guests — a girl who could not only cook and entertain but who could also outfish most of them, and that without trying real hard, or drink them off their camping chairs, with even less effort on her part. In between the gigs, we travelled from river to river in my camper, living outside, simply but well, coming into towns only to resupply and do laundry, true trout bohemian-style, making the 'disappearing act' not into a weekend getaway but a lifestyle choice. In the world where runaway insanity is the new normal and the politics the unchanging theatre of the absurd, with endless lies and fake news as their daily currency, this going incognito and incommunicado, unplugged, off the grid and back to nature was a potent antidote and a vestige of common sense. Not an escape from anything but a return to what's real and true.

For weeks, we lived to the calendar of weather and trout, keeping flexible and mobile to always be where the fishing was best, something I had done many times before but never with someone who could fully understand it, who would actually favour this way above all others. This was a total immersion in the river world of trout and all that it has to show us, a life pared down to its basics, spartan in its simplicity. Neither of us had ever been happier.

Jennifer's fly-fishing progression in New Zealand, though happening on somewhat fast-forward and full intensity pace, mirrored a typical journey of a new angler here — from the initial overconfidence to a humbling crash when expectations and skills met the reality of our trout fishery, to a steady improvement from there, polishing all those little details that so acutely add up to

make a difference between honest trout hunting and just walking the banks scaring the fish.

These are the stepping stones along the way to fly-fishing mastery — mastery not as a level or destination but as an attitude of enquiry, curiosity and constant learning — things so seemingly trivial like how we carry the rod and how quickly and directly we can deploy the cast without tangling up. How to be accurate to within inches and how to cheat your way if you are not, how to pick the line off the water without frightening every living thing in its radius and how to place your backcast in a clear gap between trees. How to adjust your casting arc so that you can fish while being down on your knees, in tall grass, with obstacles around you and tricky current lines ahead. How to place a window of drag-free drift over a fish so that you rarely have to mend and risk moving or sinking the fly. How to loosen up your cast so it's playful and light and you can deploy it in any direction you need, how to use side-pressure on the fish once it's hooked and how to move with the game so that the fighting trout is never directly downstream of you, using the full strength of the current to its advantage.

Little things and a lot of them but then, beyond the basics, fly-fishing is all in the details and not knowing them, and not having them in one's repertoire of skills, has been the cause of untold frustrations and despair, and many a ruined holidays and shattered trout dreams. It's like going fishing with not enough flies to cover the possible scenarios. In fact, I'd rather go to a river with fewer flies and more skills. New Zealand trout rarely present themselves in golf-course-type environments. We have to meet them where they are and with all the skills we can muster. Otherwise, as I like to say, we are not really 'in the game'.

Though I'd often praise Jennifer's improving skill set and solid conversion rate — and no question there: positive feedback worked a whole lot better here than any fault finding — it was Maya who bestowed her with the ultimate accolades. A true trout hound, while fishing Maya is always on the front line of all the action, at the angler's heel, coiled like a spring and hair-triggered by the slightest strike of the rod, rise or splash. This is fly-fishing with 100 per cent focus, pure and intense, where any moment could result in a fish and for the life of her she would not want to miss it.

From the earliest days, this was the way Maya started to fish with Jennifer, the only problem being that, back then and despite all the intensity and focus, there was not much happening. Certainly nothing to miss. This resulted in a rather dramatic parting of their ways.

During one of our hosted trips, I was upstream with my guys and Jennifer took Maya with her to fish a couple of kilometres below the camp. Maya was her usual intense self for a good few hours, which was about how long it took Jen to get her first fish.

'So finally I hook this big brown, for me it's huge, over five pounds,' Jennifer recalled, 'and Maya is besides herself with excitement, and I'm yelling at her to stay out of the way which she does, and then the trout smokes off into the trees and pings me off.'

It transpired that her Colorado tippets were just not strong enough to muscle with a fish of this size.

'So, I'm shaking and close to tears,' Jen went on, 'and Maya, once she realised what happened, just took one look at me, turned around and headed straight for the camp! I mean, she'd literally abandoned me on the river! I called and called her, and she turned back once and then trotted off. She was like: "Naw, fish ain't gonna happen here, sleeping is a lot more exciting alternative." And so she went back all the way to the camp on her own, and slept under the truck until I got back. Now, I pick up the rod to go fishing she doesn't even get up!'

This, I'm happy to report, is the thing of the past and my trout hound has become once again Jennifer's inseparable follower and partner in action. Only that now this following, if not quite

Since I too love to see and hear Jennifer catch fish she usually ends up catching more than me, a fact that has not gone unnoticed by Maya.

adoration, is based not on faith and hope but on frequent visual and vocal engagements with the trout. Since I too love to see and hear Jennifer catch fish she usually ends up catching more than me, a fact that has not gone unnoticed by Maya. When river and fishing gear is involved, she won't leave Jennifer's side now, as if attached by Velcro, all senses quivering with anticipation. Just occasionally, she looks up to me to see if I might be doing something she does not want to miss out on.

All the elements — our riverside *ménage à trois*, our trout-hunting teamwork and Jennifer's evolution as an angler in New Zealand — came together in a grand finale one early-summer day on our favourite backcountry river. The river is too well-known to name as it already gets more attention than it can handle, but still when the piscatorial stars align there — which means a sunny day for spotting trout, decent feeding activity and a certain absence of other anglers — the fishing can be sensational, though it can never be expected or taken for granted when it does happen.

But, with some thoughtful strategising and a lot of luck, this was one of those days. Walking from one fish to the next, and with not another soul in sight, we felt like some Adam and Eve in trout paradise, with no snake to mess things up, but with a loyal and helpful dog to help them along.

It was Maya who alerted us to an aggressive rise in the large oxbow backwater where, soon enough, over the sandy bottom we saw a huge trout. Its shadow was so black and sharp we could see the fins along its outline, but it was the size of both the shadow and its owner that made the biggest impression. Though it was difficult to judge from this far away, the trout seemed around three feet long, a sure double-figure and by a healthy margin. Leisurely, it slurped a couple more insects as we watched, transfixed.

I laid out a passable cast, straightened the line and the tippet with a measured pull and we all waited. The fish saw my big dry fly from a couple of metres away, rose confidently and . . . refused.

There was another large moth on the water, clearly visible against the metallic sheen, still alive and paddling with its feet, sending out tiny concentric ripples. Suddenly, in the mirror-like surface a crater opened up right under the fly and instantly the moth vanished in the vortex.

I heard Jennifer gasp.

'Did you see that?'

None of us could miss it. At our feet Maya was quivering, right front paw up, the long black nose pointing to the rise.

'It's too far for me,' Jen said. 'You go!'

I laid out a passable cast, straightened the line and the tippet with a measured pull and we all waited. The fish saw my big dry fly from a couple of metres away, rose confidently and . . . refused.

I withdrew the line, as gently as a surgeon pulling out a suture. I changed the fly to another irresistible dry and recast it, this time in a more relaxed way, even adding a little parachute action to the falling fly.

The huge trout was immediately attracted by the plop. It came fast and with confidence, and just as decisively rejected the fly.

'Oi! I think he knows something's up,' I said.

After the second cast the fish disappeared, and I assumed it was not so much spooked, just moved out from a known danger.

There were other smaller fish rising along the edge of the backwater and I turned my attention there. A few minutes passed in watching and getting into new positions. Jennifer stayed where she was.

'He's back! Just took another dry!' she cried out, already peeling off the line from her reel. I saw the giant fish over the sand again; perhaps he was not spooked after all.

It was a long cast, but Jennifer was as if in a trance. No hesitation, no performance anxiety, no buck fever. She shot out the line and it hit the water just perfectly, fly first and with just enough of a plop. The fish was there in a flash and this time it did not refuse.

There was a snap of the jaws, a scream, the line coming taut and shedding a spray of water, a huge splash, then nothing.

'Did you see that! Oh my Gawd, DID YOU SEE THAT! He took it, he totally took it!'

'What happened? Did he break you off?'

'No, the fly is still there. It just pulled out.'

Meanwhile, Maya was paddling around the backwater, looking for the fish, acting all serious and purposeful, coming to help her best fishing buddy, to undo her misfortune. I didn't call her back, we all need to feel important sometimes.

Instead, like so many times before, I held Jennifer in my arms until her body stopped trembling.

'This was an incredible cast,' I crooned. 'Just perfect! No one could have done it better!'

'Really? You mean it?'

'Absolutely! You've really made the grades now, not just the preschool but the trout university as well.'

She was laughing now, her body relaxing.

'Man, I so would have loved to land that fish,' she said.

'Yeah, me too!' I said. 'If you did, I'd be on a lifetime supply of triple-wood Laphroaig from your dad!'

She laughed again.

'It was the biggest trout I'd ever seen,' she said.

'And hooked!' I said. 'And you know what's the best part about it? You'll remember this fish forever, not because you caught it but because you didn't. Besides, it just means we're going to have to come back.'

'I so want to come back that I don't ever want to leave,' Jennifer said.

But leave we would, and come back, again and again. Though no reliable medical test for this is available as yet, I'm sure we both have a fair amount of trout water in our blood. The way some people are affected by the pull of the moon, we always respond to the gravitational influence of the trout waters, wherever they might be.

The first time I saw her she was only a week old, a fist-size fur ball, black, and blind and smooth like velvet. There were eleven of them in that litter, all identical siblings, except for Runty who was just as identical, only smaller. Mostly they slept, cuddled up in a pile of bodies, which bristled with big stubby noses, legs stretched in every direction and ratty tails shaped like question marks. Or they clustered on their mother's belly, oversized ticks literally sucking the life out of her, their front feet kneading the swollen teats to squeeze every last drop of milk.

Meisha, the mother, was graciously stoic throughout it all, lying stretched out on her side until, one by one, the little devils dropped off into a full-belly coma. She would then lick clean their faces and butts, never missing nor favouring any one of the pups, and she did that so, well — doggedly — and frequently, that the yucky waste accumulated in her own body and found one outlet through her eye ducts, until her thoughtful Airedale face ran with permanent crusty tears which reappeared no matter how often I cleared them. The pups either slept or fed, only occasionally squabbling and raising small hell in high-pitched whiny voices, already starting to nibble at each other, which at this age, and for the next few interminable months, would be a sign of affection. All in all, it was your average litter of purebreds, impossibly cute and so desirable there was a long waiting list of prospective owners. There was absolutely no indication that, within only a few months, and without any training but for basic obedience, one of the pups would become the best fly-fishing dog you could ever imagine. A dry-fly prodigy. A natural.

As I mentioned, there was a long list of expectant owners — a wait of a year or two to get an Airedale pup is not uncommon — but I managed to bypass it due to my sadly preferential circumstances. Only a couple of months earlier I lost my first Airedale Mops. She was hit and killed by a car in a pile up of coincidences that was impossible to either foresee or prevent and this turned me into something of a dog-less orphan, which among the 'Airedale people' is about as tragic a calamity as can befall a human being. I wrote about this in detail in *The Trout Diaries*, a farewell to the best dog that ever was, gone far too early before even reaching her prime years, yet — as it turned out in hindsight —

I wrote about this in detail in The Trout Diaries, *a farewell to the best dog that ever was, gone far too early before even reaching her prime years . . .*

only to make room for one that was unimaginably better.

I'm sure other dog breeds have their loyal fan clubs too, but the Airedale community is especially tight, active and motivated. They regularly fundraise and so always have spare cash to instantly buy out any unwanted Airedale that shows up in ads, pounds or online auctions; they rescue and rehome the dogs, cover their vet bills and flights. At times, they seem to also rescue heartbroken Airedale owners. I know this for a fact as I happened to be one of them.

I visited the pups a few more times and as soon as the prescribed seven weeks were over I brought mine home. I named her Maya and from the very beginning it was clear she was no ordinary mutt or a poodle-face show dog. For one, she had no inherent fear of anything: fireworks, thunder, lightning or gunfire — sounds and sights that can turn many dogs into nervous wrecks, pacing and panting in a panicked frenzy — elicited no more than a head cocked to the side in curiosity. Then, true to her otterhound genetic inheritance, though without any encouragement on my part, she took to water as if it was her natural element. Soon after that, she discovered fly-fishing and the mesmerising quality of moving water.

Before I go on, you need to know a thing or two about Airedales. They are — and, of course, I'm totally biased — dogs like no other. They are clowns at heart, but they are also incredibly tough and, if such things can be measured and believed, have the second strongest jaw grip after a pit bull. When an Airedale feeds, bones the size of your fingers snap like matchsticks. If you want a doormat, an adornment, a servile work dog or show pony then an Airedale is definitely not for you. As various breed factsheets point out, Airedales are alert, high-energy dogs, smart but often extremely stubborn and independent. They are not aggressive but fearless, meaning they never start a fight but they can always finish one, and they take no BS from anyone and this includes their owners.

One trait compendium warned: '. . . rough handling and punishment will get you nowhere. Hard or abusive training methods will bring failure because the Airedale is truly tougher than any trainer.' It goes on to say that an Airedale makes a totally devoted companion, but in return it fully expects to be an equal in your life, working *with* you not *for* you, a partner not a servant. Above all, it craves active human interaction, needing as much mental stimulation as physical activity. To this end, I thought, what better way to fulfil all those needs than taking the dog fly-fishing? As much physical exertion as you can take, and no shortage of mental challenges.

I don't remember exactly how and when this began, but sometime early in her first year Maya started to point rising fish for me. I never taught her that, or even thought it possible, so in a true Airedale fashion she must have figured it out herself, the cause and effect, the work and the rewards. Her logic would have gone something like this: ring on the water = (not always but often) the exciting singsong of the reel and the fish jumping and splashing on the surface = (not often but still often enough) a dinner.

By way of positive reinforcement so recommended for Airedales, and sometimes simply because we'd run out of food in the bush, I would feed her with a carefully selected fish, not too big, not too small, dispatched with respect and by *ikejime*, filleted and cubed, and sometimes — despite all that — still flapping.

Maya has never quite become a convert to catch and release of trout, though, strangely enough, many times I've seen her do that with rabbits. She'd run them down and nab them soft-mouth, then put them back on the ground, sometimes even nudge them with her nose, as if to say: 'That was fun! Go on! Let's do it again.' But with trout, it was never like that. With trout she meant business. Every time I'd release a fish, her body language would say: 'Wait! WAIT! What are you doing? Don't! No! NO! Don't do it! Don't let it go! . . . Oh man!' Then, as the fish streaked off, Maya would pounce after it, until it got too deep, then turn around and give me the 'what did you do that for?' look.

And I'd always say, 'Let's go find another one,' and she'd already be up ahead, looking for it.

We've fished like that for years, to a point I could not imagine fishing without her. She's matured and settled, and become an even better dog, and I, wary of past experiences, have taken extreme care to protect her from all motorised traffic. I've adjusted where I fish, developing a new geography of dog-friendly or at least dog-neutral rivers, and shunning all national parks (where dogs are explicitly forbidden), reasoning that I'd rather not fish a place than do it without my dog.

If Airedales need human interaction, then Maya got all of it as we've been together 24/7 pretty much since the day of her arrival. Every night, she has slept next to my bed, and sometimes on it, when I wrote she lay curled up at my feet, partly asleep but also alert to the slightest signal that the work was over and we could play. Then we would go for a run or a mountain-bike ride, to clear the mind and move the bodies, and she would streak off after rabbits and always come back, finding me without fail. In winter, I took her backcountry skiing — hiking up mountains and skiing down them — and while we humans tried to make our downhill ski tracks as sensuous and full of curves as possible, Maya's line was always straight, like a path of a stone rolling down the mountain.

Over the years, she has weaselled her way into all my books, the non-fishing ones as well, into magazine and newspaper stories, on to the cover of a mountain clothing catalogue. Even some of my regular fishing clients demand outright that Maya comes on our trips. One guy even said, 'If she can't come I'm cancelling.' And so, as always, she came, and spotted fish for us (the obvious rises anyway), and played her part of the jester, and somehow miraculously, despite her frantic excitement at every hook-up, she has never ever caused anyone to lose their fish, although a few times it was close.

Yet, apart from her unbridled excitement at seeing fish either rising or jumping when hooked, her clownish disposition and other idiosyncrasies, it is Maya's undying fascination with staring into moving water that is both the most puzzling and endearing. She never tires of it. Perhaps you can relate?

After a full day's fishing, when we finally make it back to camp, she would eat her dinner then go to find a good vantage point on the riverbank and never take her eyes off the water until it gets too dark to see. And if the dinner is a meaty bone she would take to the river's edge and eat it there, front paws clasping the bone, those hyena jaws working methodically, while her eyes scan the river for any sign of rising trout. This may be her take on eating in front of a TV but perhaps also a hint that the fearless Airedale may harbour one little fear after all, and it is one of missing out on action: a fear that a fish may rise and she would not see it, and missing out on seeing the trout rise is like missing out on life itself. So many times I've found myself joining her in this evening contemplation, gazing at the river and letting it work its magic, not wanting to miss out on Life either.

We've had our share of close calls, too — like the couple of times I had to speed-wade in to pull her out from under a strainer when she picked a wrong place to cross and would have surely drowned — but overall not many because on a river as in life I navigate by the rule that f**kups are a lot easier to anticipate and circumvent than to fix after they were allowed to happen. Still, some things you just cannot anticipate.

One time we were fishing in Reefton backcountry and the river gorged in on us and the only way ahead — short of swimming the deep pools above — was to climb up and around the canyon and descend into more open glades upstream, 'a fly-fishing paradise', as a friend described them to me. I was humping a rucksack with full backcountry kit and several days' food for both of us so it was slow going climbing up a steep face of forest mulch, studded with rocks and overgrown by ferns and bracken. Maya, as she usually does in a country she does not know, was close at my heel, perhaps a little too close.

At one point, high above the river, I reached out for a handhold above my head and it came loose out of the mulch as I touched it, about the size of a Swiss ball and ready to roll down on top of us. For a moment I balanced it on my outstretched hand, trying to push it off to the side and away from us, but the boulder was too big and too heavy and it forced my hand down, brushing past me and taking out Maya who was right below me.

I heard a long feverish yelp of agony as the two rolled and tumbled down and out of sight and then all went deathly silent.

'Maya! MAYA!' I cried, sliding on my butt and backpack down the runnel the boulder had made through the ferns. I was sure she was killed. The rock was bigger than her and several times her weight, and together they went down a long way towards the river.

At the bottom it was like looking through an avalanche debris of ferns, rocks and composting forest. I could not find her anywhere. Then I had a sudden sense of someone looking at me and as I rose to meet the gaze I saw her sitting on a river rock, shaking uncontrollably. I hugged her, wiping my eyes dry with a forearm sleeve and started to examine her for broken bones — legs, ribs, spine and hips. All seemed fine; she only had a big gash on her head and was limping badly on a front leg.

We were several hours from the trailhead, where I stashed my mountain bike, then a few more kilometres' ride to the camper, and so coming back to it was a minor epic. I had to carry her through several river crossings and help her come down from fallen logs as her front legs would collapse when she put her full weight on them. We made it back after about four slow hours and Maya appeared totally beat up and in pain, and when an Airedale is showing pain it must be severe.

That night, I was on the phone with a close friend, a vet, asking her for advice on what to do.

'Make her safe and comfortable, and see how she's doing in the morning,' she told me. 'Call me then and we'll make some decisions.'

But the next morning — a miracle if I ever saw one — Maya got up as if nothing had ever happened. There was no pain, no limping, not even a memory of it, but for that gash on her brick head. She ate, and ran, and when I picked up my fishing gear, only to reorganise it, she broke into her bouncy 360 spins, which is how she expresses her highest level of excitement. She was ready for another river adventure whenever I was. And I thought, 'Thank God these things are so tough; they are like the Landcruiser of dog breeds and you wouldn't want to come out here with anything less robust.'

Fishing together like that — hiking rivers, staring into their waters, camping, sharing the last of our food or keeping each other warm through cold bivvy-bag night — we've had an untold number of 'best days ever', regardless of what the trout were doing. It seemed like we've always done it and always would. But time is a disease and none of us is immune to it.

It began with her reluctance for going on runs and bike rides and I thought maybe the pace was too fast for her now; she had never been a racer. She would still hike and fish any distance — there was no leaving her behind for this — but it seemed to take her a lot longer to recover. Skiing together, even cross-country skiing on firm groomed trails, had become a memory, sleeping her favourite pastime.

There would be mornings when she got up visibly stiff and her back legs and hips would take ages to work properly again, and she was stoic and matter-of-fact about it, just lying stretched out in the sun as if absolutely nothing was wrong. Then, one morning while we camped on the edge of a river, she jumped out of the camper, yelped, lay down again and would not get up. Not even the sight of the fishing rod, net and the backpack would get her enthused, and I sat with her much of the morning, rubbing her back and ears, trying to massage some life back into her hind quarters, and my throat was choking up at this sudden realisation that our days together, fishing and otherwise, were slowly but irrevocably coming to an end.

It was Jennifer who brought me back from this edge of premature grief and into reality again. She has always had dogs, her entire life, usually the strays, and rescues and the 'unadoptables'. She has given them love and care, and a home to live out their troubled lives, and along the way she has seen them age and deteriorate until the moment she had to let them go.

'You need to cut her some slack,' she said. 'By our human standards she's over seventy years old. You have given her the best possible life and now she's reaching her retirement.'

Most of the time, Maya was still a pup at heart — it has been said that Airedales never really grow up — only increasingly her body, or parts of it, weren't keeping up with her spirit.

'When you get a puppy, you're getting this too,' Jennifer went on. 'We don't think about it because there is a time delay built in, ten or fifteen years. But you can't have one without the other.'

Of course, I knew that. Mops had taught me a lesson about living and mortality and this is precisely why I named the new dog Maya. In ancient Eastern traditions *Maya* means *illusion*. As the short life and sudden departure of Mops made me realise, it was an illusion to think we *have* dogs, much less *own* them. They come into our lives for a time and then they leave again, and the only part of it we have any control over is what we do with this time and what quality of life we imbue it with. The big lesson here was to make every one of the days together count because we never knew how many of them we had.

A few weeks and a disheartening number of yelping incidents later, I was selling my inflatable boat and a man and his wife came to look at it. He was an avid fly angler too, but he had hurt his back at work and so walking riverbanks was now difficult. He wanted a boat that was lightweight but sturdy and quiet as well. Since I'd converted to fly-fishing from a stand-up paddleboard, I had no need for my Zodiac any more.

The boat was an instant sell, but as we continued to talk about fishing and places I noticed they had a black Lab in the back of their twin cab. I suggested we let our dogs out so they could meet and do their thing.

The Lab tore out of the truck, jumped around everyone, then saw one of Maya's tennis balls and instantly brought it to be thrown for him to fetch. As the man did, his dog galloped after it. Maya didn't follow as she normally would. I've stopped throwing the ball for her after, one time, her back legs collapsed as she tried to chase it.

The ball throwing went on for a few more laps and the Lab was keen and sprightly, never tiring of fetching.

'You'd never tell he is twelve years old,' the woman said. 'A few months ago his arthritis was so bad he could barely walk but then the vet put him on these wonder drugs and, well, it's been like having a new dog again.'

So we are doing drugs now, reluctantly as they come with pages of small print about side effects, but meantime we too have a new dog. She tears after her tennis ball again, puts in big days on a river, and the sight of the fly rod excites her as it always has. There is no telling how much longer this will go on, as in effect we are buying her more quality time and so far this is working beyond any hopes I had only weeks ago.

I'm sure that when the time comes it'll be one of the hardest goodbyes I've ever had to say. I'm equally sure she'd want to go the way Henry Spencer wanted to go in *The Trout Diaries*, fishing until the very end, or at least watching the fish rise even if she can no longer go after them. Meantime, we live for the Now, taking it a day at a time, making every one count, or as Jennifer would say, making sure each of them is 'the best day ever'.

epilogue

OFF THE YUCATAN COAST OF MEXICO, from the prow of the skiff drifting silently over tannin-stained waters the colour of amaretto that soak the inland mangroves of the Espiritu Santo Bay, Jennifer had just laid a perfect cast with her four-inch black-and-purple Puglisi streamer and followed it up with a textbook strip-set hook-up.

'Wooo-hooo!' she yelled out. 'I'm on!'

But our guide, a shy and quiet Mayan named David, was less than impressed.

'Ay-yay-yay-yay-yay! Señora Jenny,' he shook his head, 'No no no no no!'

He took off his cap so that he could slap his forehead more emphatically.

'*Qué pasó*?' I asked. 'What happened?'

I was completely new at this game of hunting baby tarpon in the mangroves. Baby, because at this stage of their life cycle these fish were only around thirty to forty pounds.

David kept shaking his head.

'*Por el amor de Díos, Señora Jenny! Eso no es un tarpon. Eso es un cocodrilo!*'

Now I could see it too. The crocodile was a good eight feet long and now pissed at being fooled with a fly. This late in the day the only crocs David wanted to deal with were the ones on his feet. There was nothing for it but to cut the line, and quickly.

'*Vamos a regresar al lodge?*' David asked hopefully, which translated 'Shall we go back to the lodge' and meant 'I really need a drink.' Guide to guide, I totally understood where he was coming from: this line of work would be impossible without alcohol, and after a long hot and sunny day on the flats and in the mangroves, he deserved all the drinks we were going to buy him.

We were on our honeymoon and Jennifer was showing me her favourite saltwater, and her old stomping grounds, for she had lived in Mexico for nearly fifteen years. Yes, it would appear she could still make her guides want to jump off, abandon the ship and swim ashore, but it was more fun games and theatrics now. Privately, they would often say they'd rather fish with her than anyone else, and how impressed they were with her skills, especially her casting and accuracy. I could not agree more, and I got to fish with her all the time.

The fishing was easy — after New Zealand pretty much everywhere else is — but it was all new and exotic. It felt good to be a rookie again, to shed the too-tight skin of an 'expert' with all its

Keeping the boat of life light, as Jerome K. Jerome so poignantly suggested.

expectations and stigmas, to experience all new waters and species, styles and techniques and, above all, to be doing this together, taking our trout dreams global.

Our itinerary was long and ambitious — arapaima in Guyana, peacock bass in Brazil, golden dorado in Argentina, chinook salmon and sea-run trout in Patagonia, and that's only the start of it — but our approach was bohemian and, travelling in the so-called third-world countries, we could make the money go a lot further and with it buy more time, and this time together, we both agreed, was the most precious priority of all.

We also had the logistical support of Jen's father Brit, who watched our progress from afar, the way air traffic control may follow a rogue but dear aircraft, and who, from his Petitjean vise in his fly-tying room larger than most apartments, could whip up any special flies we needed and have them couriered to us anywhere in the world, prompted with but an iPhone text and a photograph.

In the big picture, our aim was to make this honeymoon last until the end of our days, not as some phony endless vacation but as a way of life, what in Costa Rica they call *pura vida* — life that is happy, simple and uncluttered by stuff but rich in experiences, filled only with essentials, in our case love and friendship, fly rods and ski gear. Keeping the boat of life light, as Jerome K. Jerome so poignantly suggested.

The way marital vows can be not just a one-off statement but a daily affirmation, the honeymoon needn't be a short-lived glitz and bust before shouldering into *lives of quiet desperation*, but more a lifestyle and an attitude. If you've read my *Trout Bohemia*, you'll know I've made an in-depth study of it. I never thought I'd get to apply its findings but then Life can unfold in a truly miraculous way, if you align with it, allow it, and follow its promptings and summons.

To this end, while we are not traipsing around looking for exotic fish, I am now also an avalanche professional, on the mountain Jennifer first introduced me to, helping to make sure the future trout water does not kill people while still in its state of pure snowflakes, and I have also learnt to row a drift boat because it's interesting and new, and that's how a lot of fly-fishing is done in Colorado.

And I make sure we always have tickets to New Zealand, and use them regularly, to return to the trout waters where it all began and to which we are eternally grateful for what they have given us.

THE END

Acknowledgements

AS WOULD BE EVIDENT from my non-fishing books and untold number of magazine assignments, I have always been more a writer who fly fishes rather than an angler who writes and so, wrapping up *The Trout Trilogy*, and my three decades of writing and fly-fishing in New Zealand, my first words of deepest gratitude must go to my editors and publishers who made it all possible.

They not only fostered and encouraged my polymathic interests but also sent me out to roam and pursue them, frequently with the help of a healthy expense account, and often based only on a brief phone call, an email and a promise that I'd deliver a useable, original and authentic story. None of them most likely ever suspected that, wherever I went and on whatever subject, I always had my fly rod with me.

Through the back-and-forth interactions of shaping the resultant narratives, of balancing and fine-tuning their ingredients and elements, these editors have also taught me how to write, praising the good, pointing out the bad and — the rarest thing of all — suggesting ways of transforming one into another: not just the bad into the good, but the good into better, and better into the best I and we could possibly make it.

This real-life hands-on writing apprenticeship most commonly took the form of the time-honoured 'carrot and stick' approach, subtle and at times not so subtle, though, since I was a quick and willing learner, over the years it became a lot more carrot and almost no stick at all, unless I really needed and deserved some.

Looking back at those formative encounters and their timelines my first and deepest thank-yous go to Kennedy Warne, founding editor of *New Zealand Geographic* magazine, who took in an enthusiastic but unskilled greenhorn and offered him an environment of a spacious and supportive literary hothouse in which to grow and develop. Among many others, he had commissioned major stories from me on both trout and salmon which, I can see now clearly from the perspective of hindsight, started me on the journey of writing about fly-fishing. Though our paths are no longer parallel and close, Kennedy's visits and the dinners and conversations that accompany them continue to be some of the brightest highlights of my social calendar and boosts of insatiable curiosity for life and adventures which he radiates.

I am equally indebted to his successors Warren Judd and James Frankham who continued this tradition of letting me live so many diverse lives, visit all the places I wanted and encounter remarkable people, and to come home to write about it all, which was like reliving the adventures all over again, only this time in a more focused and organised way, and hopefully distilling some larger and more universal truths from what happened and sharing those with the readers.

My work at the *New Zealand Geographic* has led me out into the wider world and collaborations with other editors of the highest calibre. I am especially grateful to Don Moser and John F. Ross, then at *Smithsonian* magazine, Terry Cowley at *Australian Geographic* and Bruce Heilbuth at *Reader's Digest*. Bruce, in particular, made me aware of the power of simple words and how to drive the narrative with action and suspense, and not with clever literary devices and verbal fireworks.

I also wish to thank Kathryn Webster and Jill Malcolm for their enthusiasm and lasting support for my many travel ideas, all of which allowed me to live a semi-nomadic lifestyle and to regularly do for work what most of the world does for their holidays.

Finally, I am indebted beyond measure to Caroline List and Adrian Kinnaird who have edited all my books so far, and who time and time again saved me from literary overindulgences and straight-out lapses of better judgement, and who ingeniously always made it look as if the corrections and improvements were due to my returns to common sense and never to their interventions or pointing out the obvious. Without their quiet, relaxed but fiercely no-nonsense professionalism and incredible eye for detail, *The Trout Trilogy*, and my other books, would be noticeably poorer.

As for my fly-fishing influences, they are many — and most of them you'd have read about by now in the preceding narratives — but they all began, in Wanaka all those decades ago, with meeting Ian Cole who was already a reputable guide when I picked up a fly rod for the first time. He has been a steady if infrequent presence in my fishing and in life ever since, always first to offer a joke but also there when it mattered most, like when my Airedale Mops was killed and Ian was one of the first to reach out and to literally drag me out to fish with him, until I did, despite myself and yet grateful for a friend as solid as a mountain.

Others came later but from the same ilk: Craig Smith, a man of almost embarrassingly irrepressible energy and enthusiasm, Stu Tripney and Carl McNeil — the yin and yang of masterly fly-casting, Dean Bell whose expertise can make any angler feel like a wannabe and whose directness is a challenge to my own but who shares my love for snow — the frozen trout water — and the many ways of experiencing it, including most recently the wind power of kites.

My fishing companions have been a line-up of rogues and sometimes larger-than-life characters, and thus a rich source of story-telling material. Among them, a special mention must go to Dave Witherow, who keeps the Mataura trout scared and the whisky industry in business, and still flies his microlight at the tender age of seventy-six, and the even older poet laureate Kevin Ireland who still does his best to keep up.

Michel Dedual, the chief trout scientist for the entire Taupo region, and his late wife Colette, have offered me unparalleled hospitality during all my trips to the Central North Island ever since my first visit there, on a magazine assignment in the mid-1990s. On subsequent stays, I would wake them up with the smell of freshly baked sourdough bread and we would breakfast together at the large kauri table which was the centrepiece of their family life. Then we would part for the day to get on with the various kinds of work we pursued — for me this often involved borrowing Michel's wooden boat *NeferTT*, and rowing it out to fish the Tauranga-Taupo drop-off with my dog as a companion — only to reunite at the same table in the evening for bon-vivant dinners in a true French-Italian style, with much wine, laughter, passionate conversations and Colette's inimitable culinary wizardry. I will miss those more than any fishing I'd ever done there.

From the most random encounter of watching our dogs run to each other to sniff and greet, to an even more casual 'so you do a bit of fishing?', I could not have imagined that my initial meeting with Brendan Shields would lead to one of the most profound friendships I have known. Brendan is an angel of a man, on a river as in life, and spending time with him, from our ritualistic early-season campouts to the last of the autumn mayflies in Southland, are always the high points of my trout year.

I can only wish I'd met Jennifer's parents Brit White Jr. and Sherry Odenthal a lot earlier — perhaps to show them the best of what I know in New Zealand the way they shared their favourite Colorado rivers with me — but at least now we are more than making up for those lost years with the intensity and depth of our river time together. I foresee many more such days, following the hatch calendar, sometimes putting away our rods to watch the *Pteronarcys* salmonflies coming out of their shucks on willows' new growth, and flying off like overloaded helicopters, only to be intercepted by dive-bombing woodpeckers. Or standing side by side midstream, in contented silence and the view of Mt Sopris, casting streamers on double-handed rods and pulling back the casts just before the far bank, especially that now, after so much flailing around, my Spey is just coming good and snagging up in the trees on the opposite bank has become a real possibility.

For the past fifteen years, my dogs — first Mops, and then Maya — have been my most frequent fishing companions since I've come to believe that — as I quoted Jim Thornton in *The Trout Diaries* — 'no man seeking a full life should have to face his fate without a dog'. Being with an Airedale is like having your own personal clown 24/7 and so their steady and cheerful presence has elevated all my days to beyond ordinary, on and off the river. Knowing them to the point of an almost telepathic communication I'm sure they don't care about any verbal acknowledgements. A regular riverside trout sashimi — a fish of just the right size filleted and cubed to ease the ingestion and prevent any choking — has been the accepted and preferred currency of appreciation for their 'work', company and antics.

I wish to convey my deepest gratitude to my sponsors, people and companies who saw enough value and contribution in my work to want to be associated with it and support me with their products. To Gordon Sim, CEO at LOOP Tackle Design, for taking me on as a member of their global pro-team and allowing me to be a part of an amazingly passionate and knowledgeable community, and letting me fish with the best rods, reels and lines there are. To Klaus Frimor, the developer and tester of these rods and lines, for his expertise, tuition and for simplifying the world of Spey for me by introducing me to the Scandi style, and to Grant Febery and Zac Dove who manage the New Zealand and Australian part of the LOOP enterprise and have been known to rescue me with overnight deliveries of lines and rod parts when the gear disaster struck.

My most sincere thank-yous to David, Jane and Michael Ellis at Earth Sea Sky Equipment, who have supported my work and adventures for the past two decades by keeping me clothed and warm in their best still-made-in-New-Zealand outdoor garments, both on the rivers and in the mountains. Thank you to Stu's Flyshop for his endless supply of top-quality flies and to Marc Petitjean for the Swiss-quality fly-tying tools and his tuition in all things CDC.

Lastly, bridging the gap between my fly-fishing and literary worlds, I wish to thank my fishing editors Hamish Carnachan at Fish & Game New Zealand, Rob Sloane at *FlyLife*, Ross Purnell at *Flyfisherman* and Russ Lumpkin at *Gray's Sporting Journal* for their continuing support, encouragements and for publishing my fly-fishing stories.

Finally, and singularly — though here the words can fail even a veteran writer — I am grateful to the core of my being and beyond to my wife and muse Jennifer White. Thank you for your courage and vim, and for showing me a whole new dimension to being on the river, one I had an inkling it existed but which I'd never even touched before I met you. *The Trout Trilogy* may be over, but our adventures together are only just beginning.

Derek Grzelewski
Basalt, Colorado

FROM REVIEWS FOR

THE TROUT DIARIES

'Rarely has a book received so much universal praise as Derek Grzelewski's *THE TROUT DIARIES*.'
American Angler

'It is the best fly-fishing book I have read this year.'
Jeffrey Prest, *Trout Fisherman*, UK

'Beautifully written and illustrated account of four seasons of fly-fishing for trout and salmon in New Zealand.'
Gray's Sporting Journal, USA

'I can't remember reading a better fishing book. THE TROUT DIARIES will surely become a classic.'
Rob Sloane, editor, *Flylife*, Australia

'Grzelewski can write. He has perfected the art of moving quickly . . . Go with him and it may make you view your own journey with eyes shining bright. Read it.'
Carl Walrond (author of *Survive!*), *New Zealand Geographic*

'[This is a] . . . book that is set to open the world of fly-fishing to a wider audience, with its elegant prose and passionate descriptions of our beautiful country.'
Graham Beattie, *Beattie's Book Blog*

FROM REVIEWS FOR

THE TROUT BOHEMIA

'If *THE TROUT BOHEMIA* is not the best book ever written on trout fishing in New Zealand, I would like to know what is.'
Adrian Bell, *Rod & Rifle*

'Angling literature at its finest.'
North & South

'New Zealand . . . I love that place, and this book about it. I'm jealous of anyone who lives there, writes this well, and most of all, has this Bohemian trout fishing life there.'
Dave Hughes, author, USA

'Derek Grzelewski writes like a dazzling impressionist. Trout Bohemia will make you think that fly fishing was just invented, and that every river is waiting to be explored for the first time.'
Marshall Cutchin, *Midcurrent.com*

'Trout Bohemia buzzes around the topic of obsessive-compulsive fly-fishing, darting and weaving and so dangerously fascinating that you daren't look away.'
James R. Babb, *Gray's Sporting Journal*

'On the road again with dog and fly rod, Derek Grzelewski has gathered another wonderful collection of stories about love, life, rivers and trout. If you liked his *Trout Diaries* this one is even better.'
Rob Sloane, *FlyLife*